Contents

Introduction

Although various references to the *worme*, *scrue*, and *cork-drawer* appear in 17th-century literature, no one knows when the first corkscrew appeared. One of the most likely theories is that the idea came from a worm on a ramrod or cleaning rod used to draw wadding from a gun barrel. The lithograph entitled "Cork Extractors" by Sackett & Wilhelms Litho Company of New York, included in the c.1880 book *The Growth of Industrial Art*, takes a rather humorous look at the evolution of the corkscrew. In nine steps, it shows breaking off the bottle neck, pulling a protruding cork with teeth, lifting the cork with a nail, using two forks, and, finally, five different styles of corkscrews. The bottom line is that the first corkscrew, no doubt, was a rather simple device with a wood handle and a pointed and curled piece of steel. The steel was turned into the cork and brute force was used to lift the cork.

The earliest patent issued for a corkscrew was granted in 1795 in England to the Reverend Samuel Henshall. He attached a metal button between the shank and the worm. When the worm penetrated the cork, the button would contact the top. By continuing to turn the handle, the adhesion between the cork and the bottle neck would be broken. The cork could then be easily lifted. Since the first issued patent, thousands of worldwide patents have been issued to inventors seeking a better method of cork extraction, including improved buttons, ratchets, springs, prongs, clutches, levers, and even Teflon coated worms. Other inventors added a corkscrew as an accessory on multi-purpose tools, including knives, can openers, wrenches, jar openers, bottle cap lifters, and champagne cork grips. In design patents, figures of devils, bums, pigs, parrots, and owls can be found.

The myriad of corkscrew inventions gave rise to the curious habit of corkscrew collecting. Thousands of corkscrew addicts around the globe now compete for patented and unpatented corkscrews. In 1974, several collectors from both sides of the Atlantic banded together to form the International Correspondence of Corkscrew Addicts, a group that today is limited to fifty members. Their interest namely was to share in the knowledge of corkscrew finds through annual dissemination of a photo of each members' six best finds along with knowledge of the artifact. To date,

Bull's
Pocket Guide to
Corkscrews

Donald A. Bull

4880 Lower Valley Road, Atglen, PA 19310 USA

Dedication

To Hebert Allen, Fred Andrew, Homer Babbidge, Giovanni Giachin, Claude Hardy, Perry Howland, Frank MacDonald, Bob Nugent, Evan Perry, Leon Stark, Bernard Watney, and Ted Weinberg.

Bull, Donald.
    Bull's pocket guide to corkscrews /
Donald A. Bull.
        p.   cm.
    ISBN 0-7643-0793-2 (pbk.)
    1. Corkscrews--Catalogs. I. Title. II.
Title: Pocket guide to corkscrews.
NK8549.C67B86   1999
683'.82--dc21   98-52983
                                CIP

Copyright © 1999 by Donald A. Bull

Design by Blair R. Loughrey
Type set in Pepper/GoudyOISt BT/Futura Bk Bt

ISBN: 0-7643-0793-2
Printed in China

Published by Schiffer Publishing Ltd.
4880 Lower Valley Road
Atglen, PA 19310
Phone: (610) 593-1777; Fax: (610) 593-2002
E-mail: Schifferbk@aol.com
Please visit our web site catalog at
www.schifferbooks.com

This book may be purchased from the
publisher.
Include $3.95 for shipping.
Please try your bookstore first.
We are interested in hearing from authors
with book ideas on related subjects.
You may write for a free catalog.

In Europe, Schiffer books are distributed by
Bushwood Books
6 Marksbury Rd.
Kew Gardens
Surrey TW9 4JF England
Phone: 44 (0)181 392-8585; Fax: 44 (0)181
392-9876
E-mail: Bushwd@aol.com

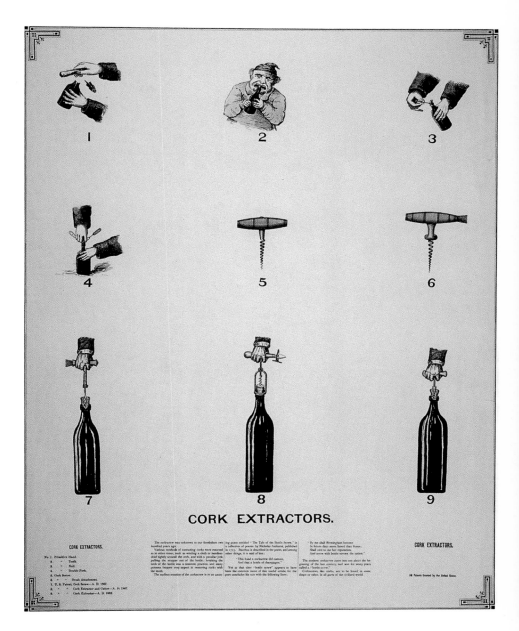

CORK EXTRACTORS.

members search desperately for corkscrews to represent their six best finds in hopes that other collectors will exclaim about at least one of them, "I've never seen that one before!" Another group, the Canadian Corkscrew Collectors' Club, now has over 300 members worldwide. Smaller organizations have been founded in France, Germany, Italy, and Scandinavia.

Where does the collector find corkscrews? Many collectors will say that the "supplies are drying up" or "there are none to be found in my area." Caution—this could be a ploy to keep you out of the flea markets and antique shows in their territory! In fact, as the interest in corkscrew collecting grows, more and more corkscrews are coming out of attics and closets and turning up for sale. Meanwhile, prices are escalating, but with some perseverance bargains can still be found. The most diligent addicts may have a bit of luck in finding an inexpensive rarity by trekking through the local Saturday morning garage, tag, or rummage sales.

Competition for corkscrews has brought about an age of the corkscrew specialist. No longer able to build a collection of all great corkscrews, collectors have resorted to picking up everything in sight in the hopes of finding "another man's treasure," which they could then trade for a particular type of corkscrew. Some collectors want only mechanical corkscrews. Others take an interest in corkscrew canes, figurals, advertising, silver ones, gold ones, folding bows, roundlets, waiter's friends, or even modern plastic corkscrews.

The popularity of a corkscrew collecting is witnessed by the growing number of books published on the subject, as well as articles written in journals, and a large number of internet websites dedicated to the topic. A search for the word "corkscrew" on the very active "ebay" auction website will turn up more than one hundred corkscrews on any given day. Although the majority are fairly common varieties, increased interest and bidding activity is inviting collectors and dealers to put up some of the rarer types for auction. For example, an English Hull's Royal Club brought $3500 while a current Warner Brothers Bugs Bunny double lever corkscrew sold for $37. A search for the word "corkscrew" on some internet search engines can turn up over 10,000 references. Alas, one must weed out the corkscrew pasta, roller coasters, race tracks, and corkscrew swamps. Searching foreign translations such as Korkenzieher, Cavatappi, Tire Bouchon, and Sacacorchos will reveal scores of additional websites. Many of the searches will find companies offering modern double levers, waiter's friends, figural, novelty, and simple corkscrews for sale.

For the truly addicted corkscrew collector, Christie's of London has semi-annual auctions with hundreds of corkscrews from the common (box lots) to the exceptionally rare. In May of 1997, a record high price of £18400 was realized for an 18th-century English silver pocket corkscrew, and a rare 1860 Philos Blake American patent sold for £9775 at Christie's April 1998 auction. In that well attended auction, over 442 lots were offered with a variety of corkscrews to suit any interest.

What does one do with collected corkscrews? Many collectors enjoy showing off their finest by opening a fine bottle of wine for a visiting friend. But only the bravest will use the rarities, which if broken, will lose considerable value. One must always bear in mind that many corkscrews were not designed to remove a tight cork from a bottle of wine. In fact, before crown caps, popping lids, and twist off caps, corkscrews were commonly used for opening bottles of beer, perfume, horse liniment, ink, medicine, cleaners, and pickles!

What is the best way to find antique corkscrews? In *Corkscrews*, Mel Reichler and Jim Egan state "Corkscrews are lost point down and found point up." So start *poking* around in antique shops—the corkscrews will find you!

Values

Value ranges are based on past sales both public and private, prices advertised in the media and at shows, prices realized on internet sales, and gut feelings. In cases where prior sale information is not readily available, value is based upon relative scarcity versus known values.

Factors that bring values down:
- Broken parts
- Missing parts
- Cracks and chips
- No markings or poor markings
- Uneducated sellers
- Apathetic buyers

Factors that bring values up:
- Two or more collectors lusting after the same corkscrew at an auction
- Over zealous buyers
- Inflation
- Low supply and high demand
- Increased awareness and interest in corkscrews

Please note that the value ranges in this book represent estimates of current selling prices of corkscrews in very good condition. Neither the author nor the publisher will be responsible for any gain or loss experienced by using the value guidelines.

Contact

If you have comments or questions about corkscrews, please write to the author at:

P.O. Box 596
Wirtz, VA 24184
USA

Part 1 *Eclectic Corkscrews*

Advertising

The corkscrew collector who specializes in advertising examples will find a very long list of available types. Barmounts, wallmounts, picnics, bows, roundlets, knives, waiter's friends, can openers, and sardine keys are just a few. Wood handle direct pulls and bell types were among the most popular in the late 1800s and early 1900s. Hundreds of different names can be found on them, but the advertising corkscrew collector must remember that he is competing for these prizes with collectors of general or specific advertising. The specific brand name advertising collector is likely to drive the prices higher than values shown in this section.

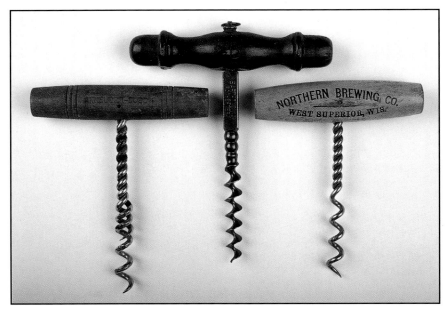

Left: "Anheuser-Busch" impressed on wood handle with double wire worm. $30-40.
Middle: "Bartholomay Rochester" stamped on square shank. $50-60.
Right: "Northern Brewing Co." imprinted on barrel shape handle with twisted wire worm. $30-40.

Left: "L. B. Co." with Edwin Walker's 1893 American patent self-pulling bell. $30-50. *Right:* "Columbia Brewing Co." with William Williamson's 1897 American patent bell. $30-50.

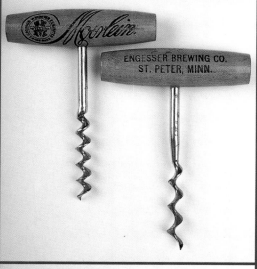

Left: "Moerlein" with web helix. $20-30. *Right:* "Engesser Brewing Co." with speed worm. $40-50.

Left: "Schlitz Brew'g Co., St. Paul" cast into the top of the button. $80-100. *Right:* "Saginaw Brewing Co., Saginaw, Michigan" on Walker wood handle with a rare instance of a notched button secured by a cotter pin. $150-200.

American Ideas

Since 1851, over 1000 American patents have been issued for designs, mechanisms, and materials used in the manufacture of corkscrews. The first was Nelson Goodyear's patent for an "Improvement in the manufacture of Indian-Rubber" and not the cork-screw. Patent titles include *Corkscrew, Cork Extractor, Cork Puller, Cork Pulling Device, Automatic Corkscrew, Cork Removal Device, Cork Ejector,* and *Electric Corkscrew.* Others fall under the main object of the patent such as *Can Opener, Bottle Opener, Combination*

Top row left to right: Curley 1884. $400-600; Chinnock 1862. $400-700; Strait 1883. $700-1200; Walker 1891 Pat. Pend. with Schlitz Globe. $150-200. *Bottom row left to right:* Bennitt 1883 marked MAGIC. $275-325; Woodman 1886. $1000-1200; Barnes 1876. $400-800; Haff 1885. $75-100.

Tool, Jar Opener, and Knife. Many cork-screw collectors limit their collections to only patented corkscrews either from their own country or selected countries. This has resulted in in-creased values for examples with patent markings.

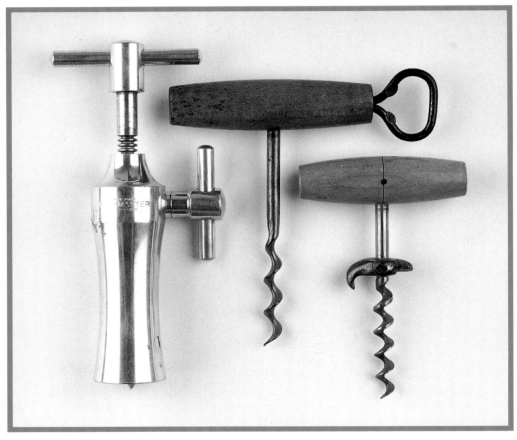

Left: McDowell 1948 "Korkmaster." $75-100.
Middle: Walker direct pull with speed worm and cap lifter. $150-200.
Right: Williamson with foil cutter and wire breaker. $25-50.

Art

Although the diehard corkscrew collector thinks of all corkscrews as works of art, there are some that should simply be classified as "Art" corkscrews. Some are poor works of art and others have a bit more interest.

Some are good ideas like outstretched arms, which make a perfect T-Handle puller. Some are not so good ideas such as a nude holding a wreath which is a bit difficult to *grasp*, although it does feel good as a cap lifter.

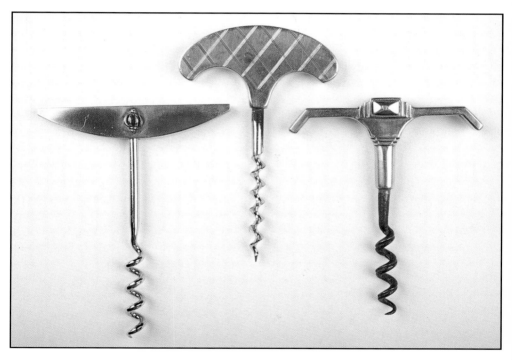

Left: 1975 Danish design by Moltke. 300 Produced. $250-300.
Middle: Towle Silversmiths, Newburyport, Massachusetts. $200-250.
Right: Wakeley & Wheeler, London, England. 1906. $350-400.

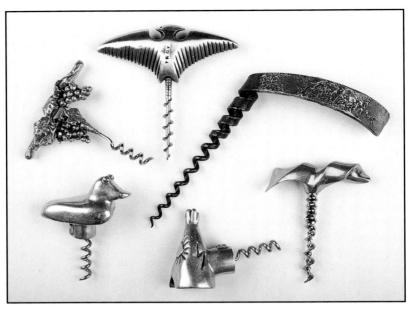

Top row left to right: Unmarked grape design. $30-40; Eagle marked TROY. $50-60; 1980s design by artist Brian Cummings. $65-75.
Bottom row left to right: Two pewter designs marked © ROUX designed by Steve Vaubel of Brooklyn, New York. $60-90; Brass twist handle marked SAMSON #4 '89. $40-50.

Various English brass two finger pull figurals. $15-50.

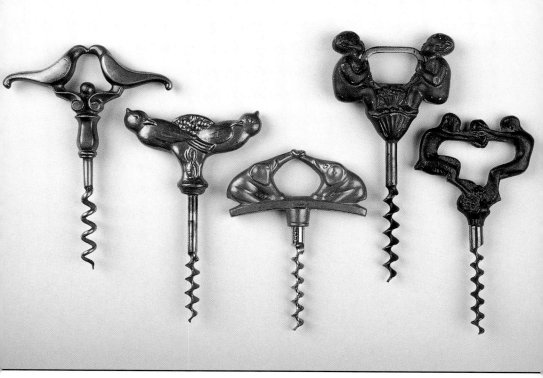

Left to right: Kissing Birds by Just Anderson, Denmark. $125-150; Doves with Grapes (DENMARK). $125-150; Dancing Elephants (MADE IN SWEDEN. C.V.H. ROSTFRITT). $175-200; Cherubs with Basket (DENMARK). $200-250; Man and Satyr Wrestling Grapes (FSG 4PR. CVH. bronze). $150-175.

Brass marked RAPID, SWISS MADE. This model has
been sold in the United States for several years in
brass and chromed versions for about $150.

Barscrews are heavy cast iron or brass corkscrews that mount on bar tops using either clamps or screws. Some are designed to remove a cork by first turning the worm into the cork, then pulling a lever. Others turn the worm into the cork and extract it in one continuous motion. A 1902 Sears catalog contains several models targeting the saloon, soda fountain, restaurant, club, and hotel market. Of all corkscrews, barscrews are those most frequently favored with names. These include Acme, Ajax, Bacchus, Blitz, Cedon, Champion, Crown, Cyclop, Daisy, Don, Eclipse, Enterprise, Estate, Express, Extractee, Famlee, Favorite, Handy, Hektor, Helios, Hero, Infanta, Invincible, Little Quicker, Meriden, Merritt, Modern, New Era, Phoenix, Pullmee, Rapid, Rimo, Safety, Samson, Shamrock, Shomee, Simple, Slam, Swift, Unique, Victor, Vintner, Yankee, Zeus, and the Quick and Easy Cork Puller.

The "Rotary Eclipse."
$1200-1500.

Barrel

The barrel functions like the more common bell or frame type corkscrews. By continuously turning the handle, the cork is lifted into the barrel.

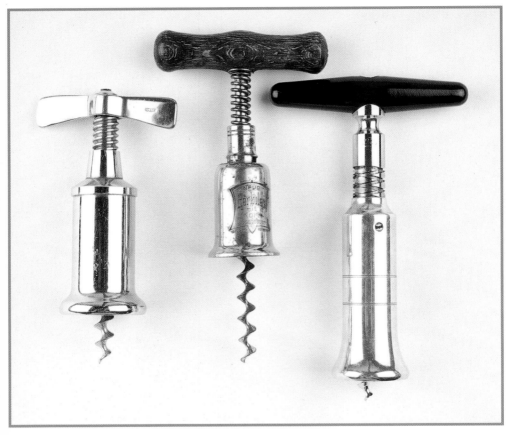

Left: Chromed closed barrel with handle marked ITALY. $30-40.
Middle: Marked NEUE HERKULES MIT KORK AUSTOSSER, D.R.G.M. GERMANY, c.1932. $100-125.
Right: Perpetual type corkscrew marked DICO, WAKEFIELD, MASS., PAT. PEND. $350-500.

Bows

One of the first bows a new cork-screw collector is apt to find is a rather simple worm that folds out from the center of the bow with the bow be- coming the handle of the cork re- mover. Hundreds of sizes, shapes, and configurations of folding bows have been produced since the 18th century.

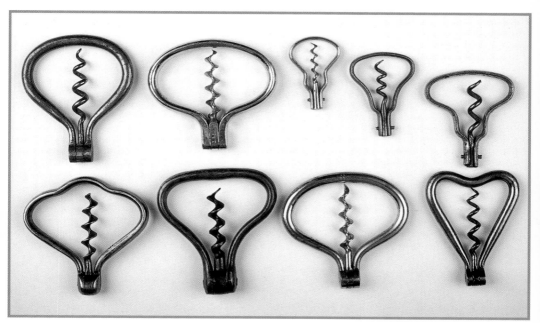

Various simple folding bows with corkscrew only. $10-50.

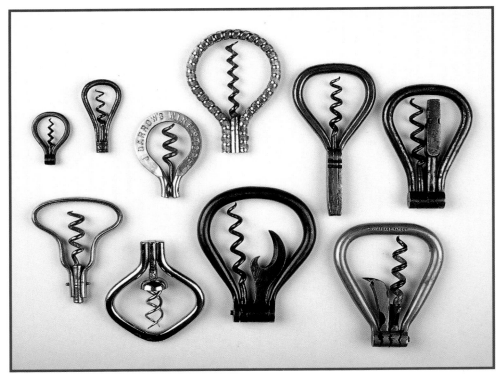

Top row left to right: Miniature. $25-50; Unusual hinge. $50-75; Advertising. $75-100; Ornate silver stipple. $125-150; Carriage key. $250-300; Carriage key and worm. $250-300.
Bottom row left to right: Havell patent. $50-100; Double helix. $80-100; Cap lifter and worm. $100-150; Foil cutter and worm. $100-150.

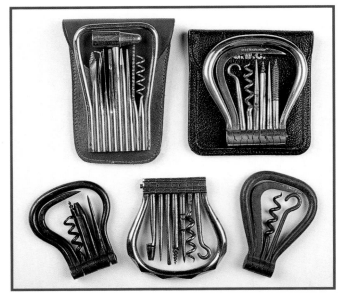

Multi-tool bows.
$50-75 per tool.

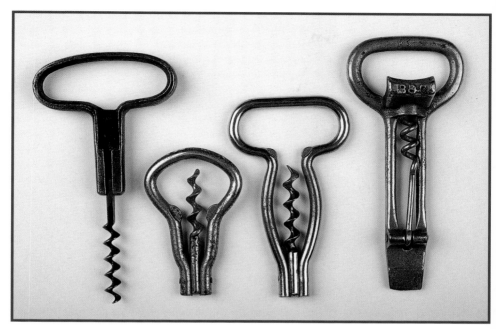

Left to right: Long channel at base.
$150-200; Cap lifter frets. $60-80;
Elongated wire. $50-60; Marked B & C
with cap lifter and lid prier. $75-90.

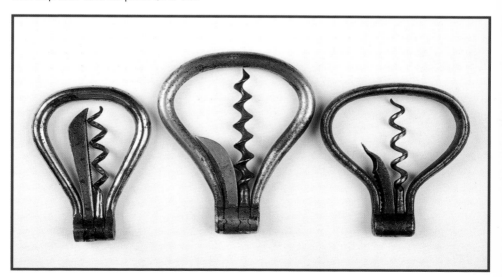

Three bows with foil cutter
and corkscrew. $100-200.

Can Openers

Millions of combination can opener/bottle opener/corkscrews have been made and sold in housewares departments in stores. Today, you can still buy them for under $1.00—New! But they aren't as collectible as the rusting lot found in these photos. If you are starting a can opener collection, your first hundred varieties will be easy and cheap. How much you are willing to pay after that will depend upon how deeply you get involved with can openers.

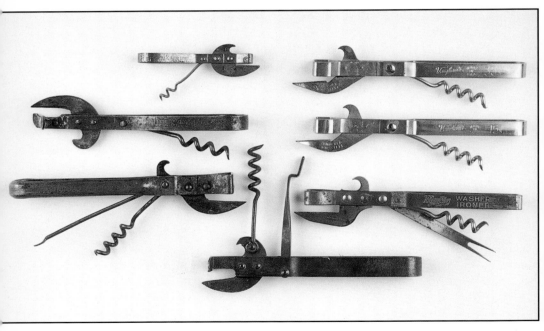

Top row: Miniature 3". $35-50; Vaughan with stamped price. $5-10.
Second row: Advertising. $20-40; Vaughan with stamped price. $5-10.
Third row: Two combination can opener/corkscrews with olive/cocktail fork. $30-50.
Bottom: This rare example does not have a can opener. It looks like a can opener, but is only a waiter's friend. $100-150.

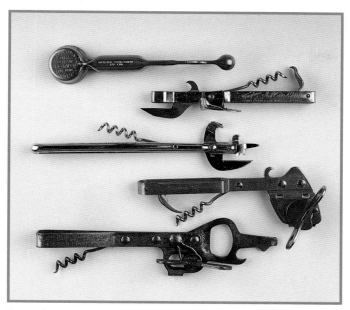

Top to bottom: Re-Cap-O. Ransom Company, Detroit. $10-15; Protective shield marked THUMB GUARD. $2-3; Basic chrome. $1-2; Vaughan's. Made by the zillions. $1-2; QUINTUPLET KITCHEN UTILITY. 1936 American design. $25-30

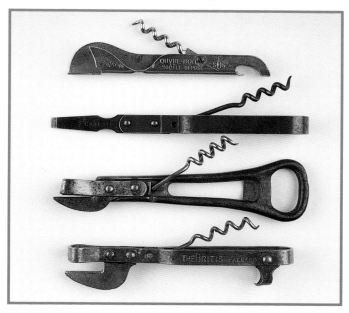

Top to bottom: A French can opener. $20-30; Screwdriver in can opener style marked CAST STEEL. $40-50; Marked HENN on a chicken trademark. $35-50; Marked BRITISH MADE PAT 11360, MADE IN ENGLAND. Frederick Sunderland's 1909 patent was for the piece on the tail end marked CROWN CORK OPENER. $30-40.

Canes & Walking Sticks

Are they real corkscrews? This seems to be one of the first questions asked about canes with worms attached to the handles and concealed in the sticks. There are stories about dealers who have taken canes with various hidden implements and changed them into corkscrews. And there are collectors who say that all threaded ones are fakes and the only genuine corkscrews canes are those with a bayonet fit. So, *are* they real corkscrews? The *answer* is simply that some were originally intended to have corkscrews and others were re-fabricated! But they are all cane and walking stick corkscrews!

A corkscrew cane will uncork a bottle and another and another, and, if you drink it all, it will help you walk home. Corkscrew cane prices vary from $400-2000 depending upon marks and design.

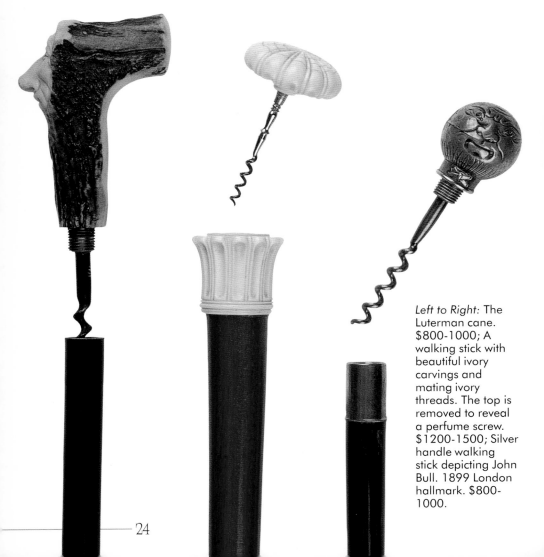

Left to Right: The Luterman cane. $800-1000; A walking stick with beautiful ivory carvings and mating ivory threads. The top is removed to reveal a perfume screw. $1200-1500; Silver handle walking stick depicting John Bull. 1899 London hallmark. $800-1000.

Carvings

A very popular artistic endeavor in America was the carving of tusks, antlers, wood, or pieces of ivory as handles for corkscrews. Most incorporate a bell cap on the shank for self pulling of the cork and most of the shanks are threaded into or pinned to the handle. Any that are simply pressed and/or glued in a hole in the handle might be suspected as fakes. The carvings normally had silver fittings on one or both ends. Values range from $250-1500.

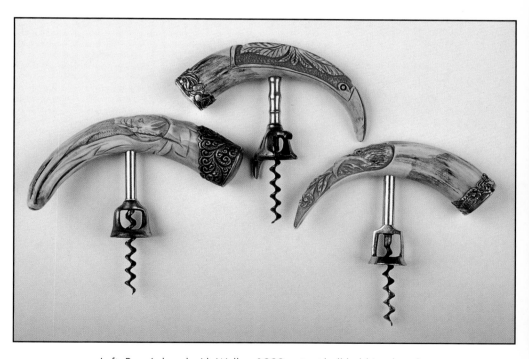

Left: Boar's head with Walker 1893 patent bell held in place by a plain hollow tube over the shank. $400-500.
Top: A floral design cut into the tusk in such a manner that it looks like the head of a Toucan. 1900 Walker bell. $300-400.
Right: Bird with long beak grasping a plant branch. $450-600.

Champagne Taps & Tools

Champagne or soda water taps are designed to penetrate the cork of a bottle containing gaseous liquid. The user opens a valve to draw off liquids and closes it to preserve the bubbles.

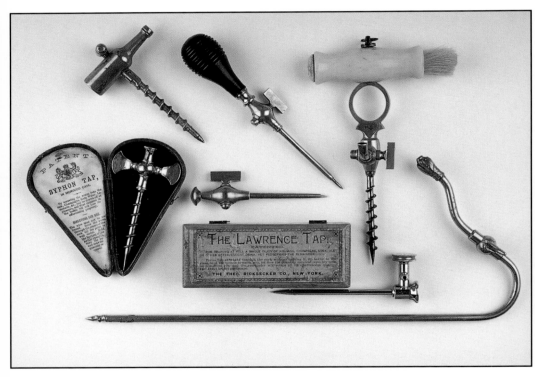

Top row left to right: "New Century" tap by Williamson Company. $50-75; Round handle two piece tap. $80-120; Bone handle with brush. Marked HOLBORN CHAMPAGNE SCREW with 1877 registration mark. $150-200. *Bottom row left to right:* Maw's Prince of Wales Soda Water Tap with case. $100-125; Abyssinian. $40-60; The Lawrence Tap by William and Richard Bentley (1876 American design) with original box. $125-150; Long French tap with serpent design spouts and valves. $150-200.

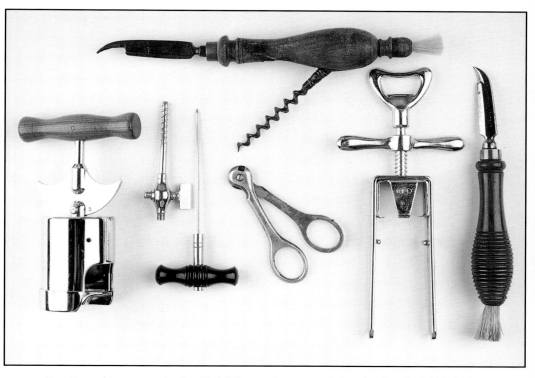

Top: Rare champagne knife with folding corkscrew and cleaning brush. $600-800.
Bottom row left to right: 1985 American patent with cam action for grasping and
lifting the cork. $30-40; 5 1/2" two piece tap. $75-100; Folding wire cutter
including a cigar clipper. $20-30; Flynut champagne cork puller. $30-50; Champagne knife with blade marked G. DOWLER'S PATENT. $150-200.

Chip Chop

Here's something to break the ice.

The Chip-Chop in original box marked DRINK-DIALER*/ CHIP-CHOP BY APEX, TRADEMARK. The bottom part of the Chip Chop has five ice crushing points, and the device is spring loaded to cushion the blow when crushing ice in the glass. $10-30.

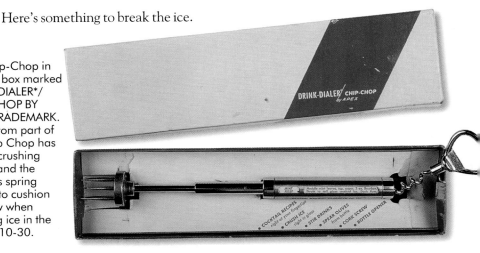

Clough Stuff

Twenty three patents for corkscrews and corkscrew producing machinery were issued to William Rockwell Clough of Alton, New Hampshire. In 1875, his first corkscrew patent was issued covering his small wire corkscrew used for medicines, inks, and other products with small corks. His last in 1920 for a "Pocket Implement" pictures a knife with a folding worm and other blades. His most successful invention was in October of 1900 for a "Machine for Making Corkscrews." Millions of corkscrews were produced with a wood sheath indicating the October 16, 1900, patent date. The wood sheath was a very popular form for all types of advertisers from breweries and distilleries, to haberdasheries, to insurance companies, and even laundries. As frequently as these types turn up, one would suspect that thousands of companies used them.

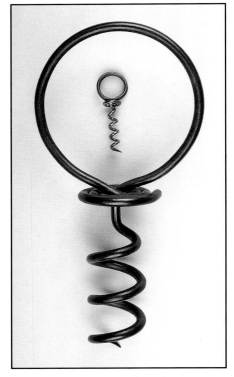

11 1/2" Clough point of purchase display corkscrew. $150-200. Normal size Clough shown in center for comparison.

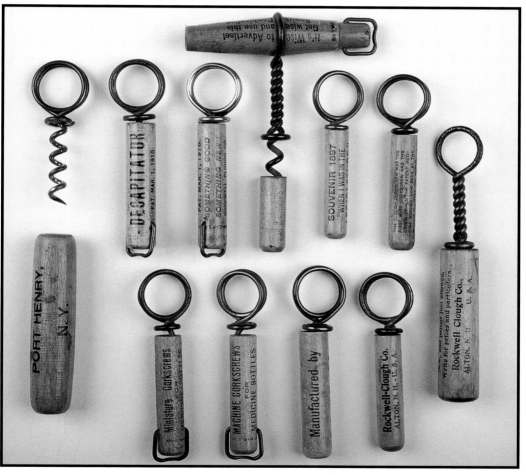

Various corkscrews used by The Rockwell Clough company to advertise their own products. Values range from $10-50.

The "All-Ways" Handy Combination Bottle Opener & Corkscrew. A. W. Stephens Company of Waltham, Massachusetts, used the following advertising copy to sell corkscrews: "One of these openers hung up in the kitchen beats a hundred of the other kind scattered on the cellar floor." $20-50 depending upon advertising and local interest.

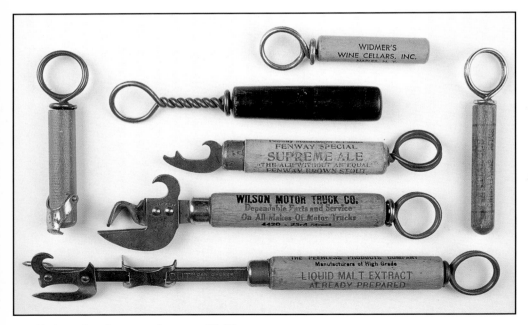

Various sheath type corkscrews. $2-75.

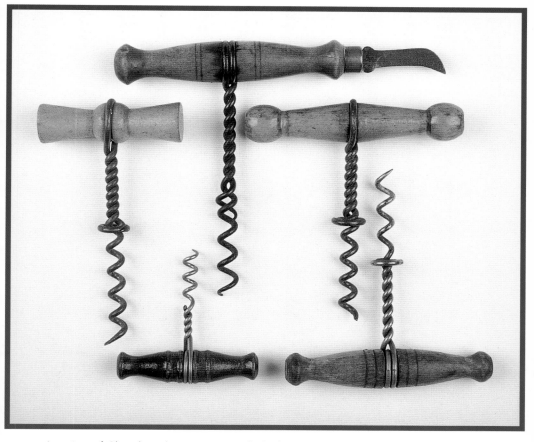

A variety of Clough corkscrews many of which were manufactured by the Williamson Company of Newark, New Jersey.
Top row left to right: Bowtie handle. $25-35; A rare un-
marked example with foil cutter. $75-100; Clough's 1899
wood handle design patent in lacquered oak. Wire finishes in
a button above the worm. $40-50.
Bottom row left to right: Midsize with 2 1/2" wide handle.
$10-15; Clough's 1876 patent. Marked WILLIAMSON'S on
top of wire wrap. 3 3/4" handle. $25-35.

William Rockwell Clough's 1876 patent for a corkscrew formed from one or two pieces of wire was manufactured by the Williamson Company. These corkscrews were promoted heavily for advertising purposes. They are found with no marks, the "Williamson" name, and various advertisements. $15-50.

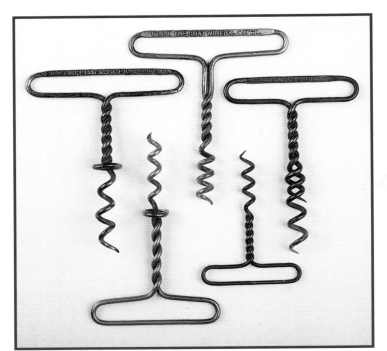

Two finger "eye-glass." $100-125; A wire type with button finishing in a hanger hook. Wire is wrapped on handle. Origin unknown. $75-100; Two finger loop "eyeglass" with wire button. $125-150.

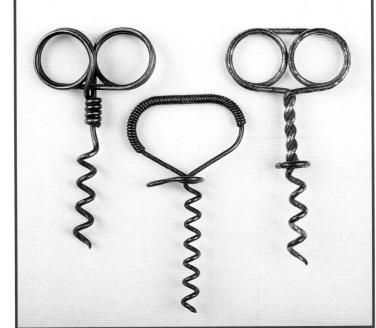

Codd Pieces

In 1870, Englishman Hiram Codd introduced an internally stoppered bottle. The bottle has a glass ball molded into a chamber in the top. A rubber "O" seats in a ring molded inside the top lip. When the bottle is filled with liquid, the pressure of the gas holds the glass ball against the rubber seal to maintain the pressure until released. A Codd bottle opener added to a corkscrew handle was a useful accessory.

Top: Boxwood handle English registration of J & W Roper of Birmingham. $100-150; A simple Codd bottle opener. $75-100; Matt Perkins 1884 English patent in marked CONEY'S PATENT. $150-225. *Bottom:* Codd bottle marked W H DIXON EAST GRINSTEAD with a wood round "opener" hollowed out and leaving a stud in the middle to depress the ball in the bottle.

Collapsing

In 1891, Carl Hollweg was granted an American patent for a collapsing corkscrew that protected the pocket from the worm. Hinges in four places allow the user to close the corkscrew for storage or fully open it for usage; the case acts as the handle. They have been produced in several sizes and shapes. Some have been used for advertising purposes. A 1913 catalog from Lewis Brothers of Montreal, a hardware wholesaler, offered this corkscrew as the "Telescope." They sold them for $2.70 per dozen.

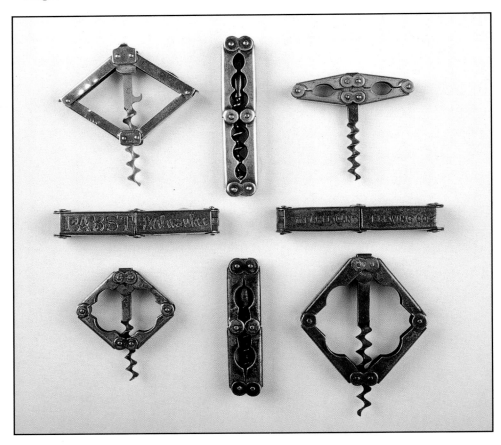

Top row left to right: Silver with a gold plated worm. Marked NAPIER STERLING. $300-500; Common 3 1/4" Hollweg. $75-85; 2 1/4" Hollweg. $75-100.
Middle row: Two with brewery advertising. $80-125.
Bottom row left to right: 2 1/4" German made. $75-100; 2 5/8" Swedish version by Hedengran & Sons. $75-125; Rarest Hollweg with one scallop on the inside of the links and a square shank on the worm. It is marked MADE ABROAD, PATENT APPLIED FOR, PATENT ANGEMELDET, MADE IN GERMANY. $200-250.

Columbus

The Columbus is an 1893 invention by Eduard Becker of Solingen, Germany. The split frame facilitates removal of the extracted cork from the worm. The spring between the handle and the frame assists the extraction by exerting pressure on the handle to gradually withdraw the cork. Becker was issued German patent 70879 in March of 1893. An English patent was issued in September followed by an American patent in April, 1894.

Left to right: Metal handle type marked LANGBEIN GERMANY. $100-150; Stag horn (8 1/2") marked COLUMBUS on one side and GERMANY on other. Trademark of Müller & Schmidt, Solingen, Germany. $150-200; Marked D.R. PATENT NO. 70879. $60-80; Root handle version marked ORIGINAL—BACCHUS at top of frame. $125-175; Argentinean version marked INDUSTRIA ARGENTINA, GAUMEN, M. REG. (for registered mark). $75-100.

Designer

Unique corkscrews were designed for a number of firms including Cartier, Christofle, Dunhill, Eloi, Gucci, Hermes, Jensen, and Wilkins. Retail prices range from $100-500.

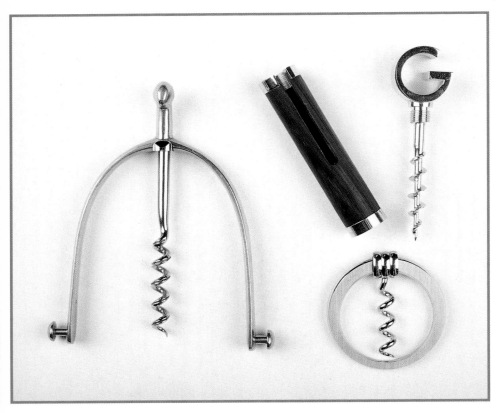

Left: Spur marked HERMES PARIS, MADE IN FRANCE, DEPOSE. $350-400.
Top right: Gucci picnic style with threaded and slotted sheath. The sheath mates with the center portion of the G. $250-300.
Bottom right: Cartier circle folding bow marked MUST DE CARTIER, MADE IN FRANCE. $350-400.

Double Lever

The Double Lever is rather simple to use and can make cork extraction a pleasurable experience. The arms are raised to expose the worm below the frame. The worm is turned into the cork, and, by simply lowering the arms, the cork is extracted.

Left to right: "A1" Double Lever patented by James Heeley & Sons of Birmingham, England, in 1888. $125-175; 1880 English Patent by William Baker also of Birmingham. $500-800; French Double Lever. $300-350; The "Eterno." Ettore Cardini's 1945 Italian Patent. $200-300.

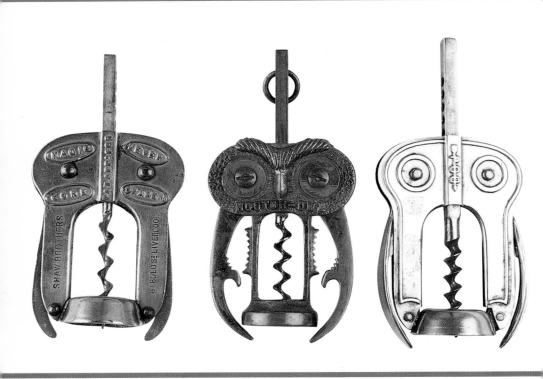

Left to right: English MAGIC LEVER CORK DRAWER. $100-125; "Hootch Owl." American Design Patent Number 98,968 of March 17, 1936, by Richard Smythe. $1000-1500; Marked BOJ (a trademark of B.Olanta y Juaristi in Spain). $50-75.

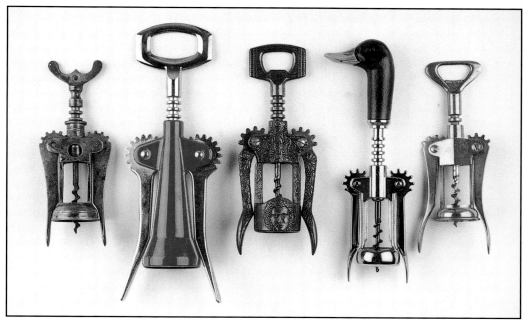

Left to right: After Dominick Rosati's American Cork Extractor Patent (1930). $25-50; Modern red double lever. $20-40; Italian designer Cipriano Ghidini's American Design Patent Number 228,613 of October 16, 1973. $20-30; Duck (*featured*), plus a dog, golf ball, and horse, with hand painted resin handle, currently marketed at $30-40; Common brass usually marked ITALY and sometimes found with advertising (also in chrome). $15-30.

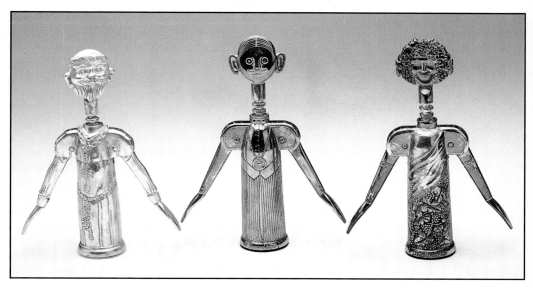

The Sommelier corkscrew in the center is pictured in Italian designer Aldo Colombo's American Design Patent Number 274,974 of August 7, 1984. The Monk Cellarmaster with cellar key hanging from his sash, the Sommelier, and Bacchus are silver plated. $30-40.

Italian aluminum double levers from the late 50s through early 60s known as the Barman, Clown, and Barmaid. The clown is the rarest of the lot. $50-90; clown $150-200.

Names such as Liesse, Hoan, Farberware, and Bar-tech can be found on modern plastic double levers by stopping in a housewares store. $10-25.

Italian Carlo Gemelli's American Design Patent Number 184,613 of March 17, 1959. The original box has this copy: "It's a giant corkscrew and bottle opener. Pulls all corks with ease! You can't mislay this one - it's too big!—light in weight—strong." $125-150.

Finger Pulls

Finger Pulls are designed to fit two, three, or four fingers. Most are English. With a couple of exceptions, brute force is used to remove the cork. I have only included metal pulls in this category. Each photo contains pulls with variations in size or design. Some are very slight. A keen-eyed pull specialist will, no doubt, be able to root out many more.

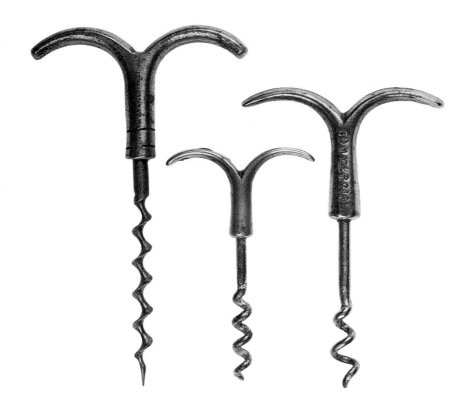

Two finger direct pull corkscrews. Unmarked $20-30. Marked varieties including C. T. WILLETTS L$^{\underline{D}}$ and COMMERCIAL. $30-80.

Two and three finger pulls with a cap lifter added. $5-50 depending upon marks.

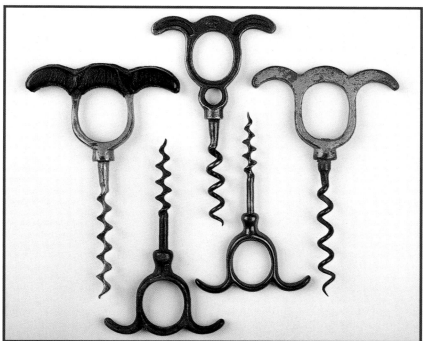

Three finger pull or "eyebrow" handles spanning 2 1/4" to 3 1/4". Unmarked plain handle examples range from $5-25; Marked handles $25-50; Leather wrapped handles $75-100.

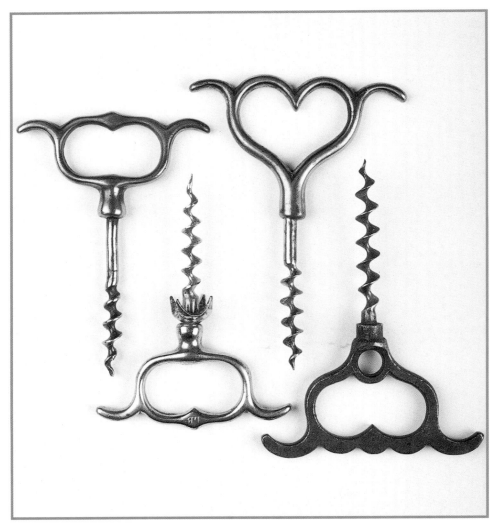

Top: Unmarked iron pull. $25-35;
Heart shape handle. $75-100.
Bottom: Teeth added above worm. Marked L B. $125-150;
For use independently or with a lever. $40-50.

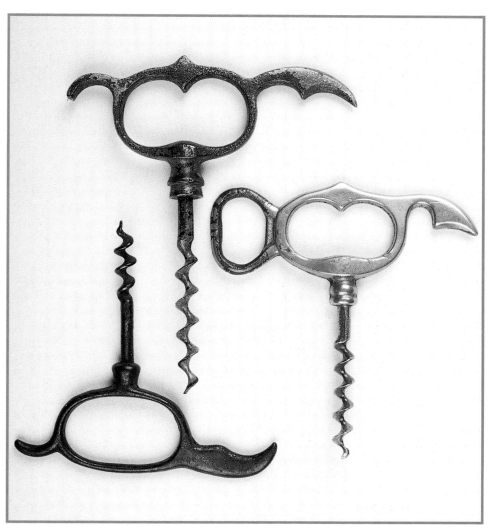

Three examples of four finger pulls with a foil cutter/wire breaker at the handle. One has a cap lifter added to the design. $50-75.

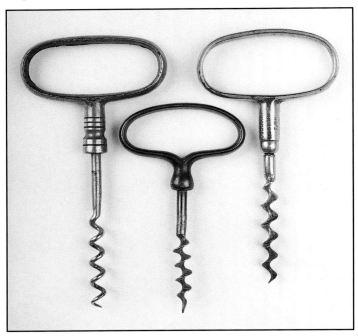

Full grip pulls are often called the "Cellarman's Cork-screw." Simple unmarked examples value $10-20. Marked examples range from $20-125 including a FARROW & JACKSON LTD LONDON mark at the upper end.

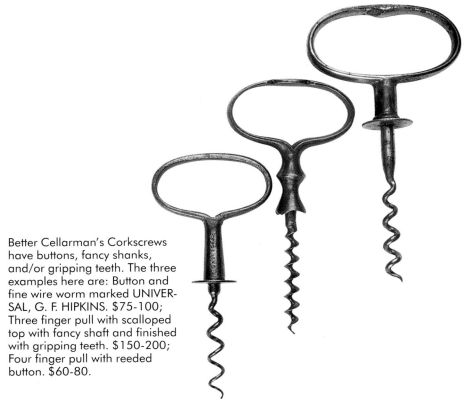

Better Cellarman's Corkscrews have buttons, fancy shanks, and/or gripping teeth. The three examples here are: Button and fine wire worm marked UNIVER-SAL, G. F. HIPKINS. $75-100; Three finger pull with scalloped top with fancy shaft and finished with gripping teeth. $150-200; Four finger pull with reeded button. $60-80.

The most common Cellarman's Corkscrews are those with a simple oval design. Various others were produced in hopes of creating a better grip or to be marketed as novelties. These examples are: Two finger one piece marked ZEITZ. $50-60; Squashed design four finger pull. $60-70; Squashed design two finger pull. $40-50; One finger, one piece knot marked STUBAIMARWA. $30-40.

Flynut

A flynut corkscrew consists of a handle with threaded shank and worm, a frame or barrel, and a "flynut." The collar of the frame is placed over the bottle neck, and the worm is screwed into the cork by turning the top handle. With the worm inserted in the cork, the flynut is turned clockwise on the threaded shaft to lift the cork out of the bottle.

In 1876, A. M. Perille of Paris, France, was granted a French patent covering several corkscrew designs including a triple stem flynut version. Perille was a prolific producer of corkscrews, and the basic flynut design was produced well into the 20th century. The simple examples marked HELICE or LA MENAGERIE are the most commonly seen.

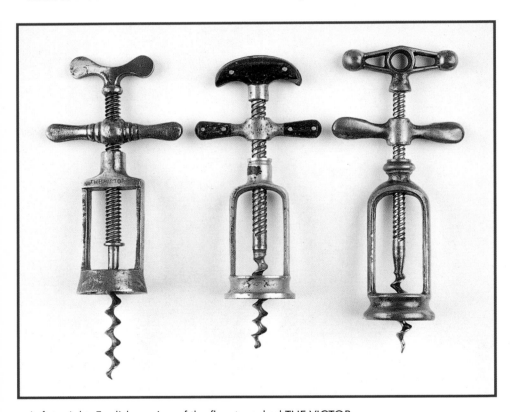

Left to right: English version of the flynut marked THE VICTOR. $150-175; Wood embellishments riveted to the handle and flynut. $100-125; Perille's "Aero" marked AERO on the flynut and JHP DEPOSE PARIS on the frame. $175-200.

Left to right: Marked J. PERILLE DEPOSE PARIS on one side and HELICE JHP
DEPOSE on the reverse. Flynut is fixed to the frame. $50-80; Cast aluminum
frame (most of this type are found with a steel frame). $50-75; Tightly wound
spring barrel. $200-250; She's a Perille type corkscrew, and she has been
perfectly fitted with head, upper body, and skirt. Each of the three carved
rosewood pieces is secured with a wood pin. The head is secured to the
handle at the top, the upper body to the fly nut, and the skirt to the frame.
The bottom of the skirt is marked "Made in France." $100-200.

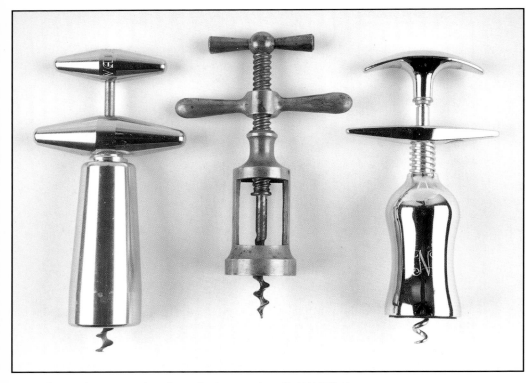

Left to right: Brass colored, marked on top handle VALEZINA. Patented in England, in 1943, and in America, in 1944, by American inventor John Miller. $100-125; Brass Italian version of the flynut corkscrew. Marked EDWIN JAY MADE IN ITALY. The marking is on top of the center hub of the flynut, which is an unusual, inconspicuous spot for an Italian corkscrew. $75-100; Hour glass barrel made in Spain. $50-60.

Frame

Corkscrews with open frames have been made with a wide variety of "better mousetraps" to pull the cork or remove the cork from the worm. The bottom of the frame is flared. In some instances, the frame is placed on top of the bottle before turning the worm into the cork. In others, as the worm is turned into the cork, the frame descends to meet the neck. Continuing to turn the handle, unlocking the handle then turning, turning a secondary handle, and reversing the rotation are different methods employed to lift the cork into the frame. With the open frame, the cork can be grasped as needed to remove it from the worm, if there is no mechanical means of doing this.

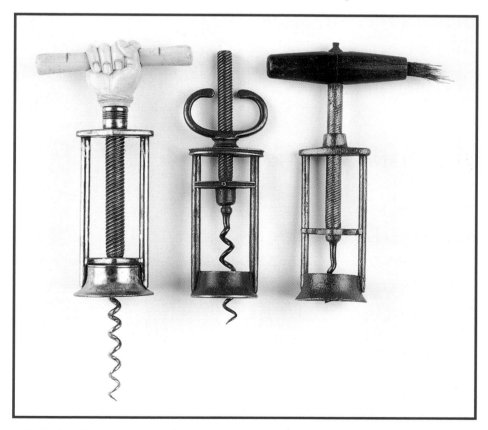

Left: Early 19th century two pillar frame with ivory hand gripping bar. $2000-3000.
Middle: Open frame operated by grasping the frame and handle to insert the worm into the bottle. The handle rotates freely on the frame and is turned to lift the stem and guide in the frame, extracting the cork. Reverse the handle to lower the worm and remove the cork. $1200-1500.
Right: John Coney's 1854 English patent with a threaded stem passing through a two post frame. $700-1000.

Left pair: "Farrow and Jackson" type unmarked butterfly
handle corkscrews with centering button. $150-250.
Third: The "Excelsior." Armand Guichard's 1880 French
patent. $250-350.
Right: The "Diamant" based on an 1876 French patent
by Jacques Perille. $250-350.

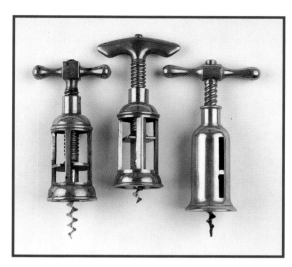

Left to right: Four column brass frame with handle marked ITALY. $70-80; Four column brass frame with square centering device. $80-100; Slotted barrel marked CAPPELI, BORGOMANERO. $150-200.

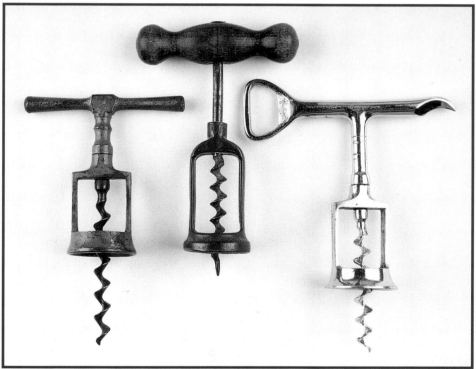

Left to right: George Willet's 1884 English registration, THE SURPRISE. Copper plated. $75-100; Unmarked European version of the American Chinnock patent. $40-50; 1922 English design including a cap lifter and wire breaker. $150-200.

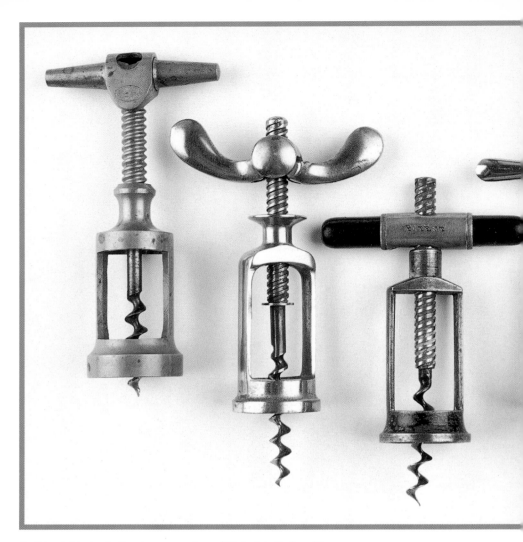

Left to right: An Italian brass version of Heinrich Ehrhardt's 1891 German registration with locking handle. $60-80; The "Bodega," an 1899 German patent by Ernst Scharff. $500-600; Marked PATENT and G. R. on the brass sliding collar lock. This is another example of Heinrich Ehrhardt's 1891 German registration. $200-300; The "Challenge." $35-75; The "Wulfruna." Stephen Plant's 1884 English patent. $150-200.

Left: Locking handle frame marked MONOPOL WEST GERMANY on the handle. It has a left-hand worm and comes in a box that indicates it is a left-handed model. Instructions on the box, however, are for a right-handed model. $30-40.

Right: Locking collar with closed barrel. Box labeled: "'Lifetimer' Automatic Cork-Puller, copyright by gadgets of California, 'The gift for a lifetime'." $40-50.

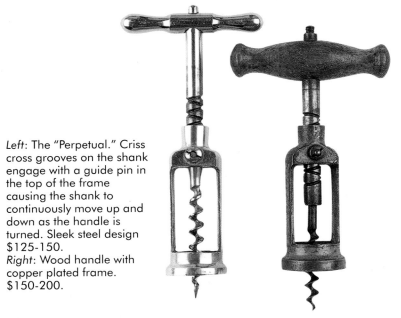

Left: The "Perpetual." Criss cross grooves on the shank engage with a guide pin in the top of the frame causing the shank to continuously move up and down as the handle is turned. Sleek steel design $125-150.
Right: Wood handle with copper plated frame. $150-200.

In 1901, Ernst Scharff registered a design in Germany for a frame corkscrew with an enclosed bearing at the top of the frame to assist in smooth extraction of the cork. G. Usbeck had a similar design in 1909 with an exposed bearing at the top of the frame. *Left to right*: Scharff design marked on frame SOLON/D.R.G.M. No 152004. $100-125; Cheap imitation stag handle. $3-4; Usbeck design. $30-40.

Funnels, Jiggers & Shakers

In a 1941 Chase Specialty catalog, the "Bar Caddy" is described as "a combination jigger, bottle opener, corkscrew, and ice breaker. The jigger is marked off for measuring 3/4 of an ounce, 1 ounce, 1 1/2 ounces, and 2 ounces. The jigger bottom is extra heavy metal, so you can crack ice cubes with it. The handle is a crown bottle-cap opener. A cork- screw is concealed inside the handle, when assembled." What more could the home bartender ask for? Such tools do turn up quite frequently at flea markets for bargain prices. Less common and more desirable are the combination tools with funnels. Many of these have been found with initials engraved or as awards given at special events.

Left to right: Napier small shaker with funnel, measurer, cap lifter, and corkscrew. $150-175; Napier "five in one" tool: Cap lifter, corkscrew, funnel, drink measure, and bottle resealer. $60-75; Sterling cap lifter/corkscrew, which appears to be a cover for a container. $65-75; Another five function tool. $60-75.

Combination
funnels, cap lifters,
and corkscrews.
$100-150.

Front left and right: Silver plated jigger with cap lifter and corkscrew marked CAM-
BRIDGE, E. P. C. 711. $60-75; Jigger with rotating handle to expose recipes. $2-12.
Middle left and right: Brass "Bar Caddy." $2-12; "Bar Boy" by Tempro Incorporated,
New Haven, Connecticut. $15-25.
Back center: Jigger has "A. M." sad face on one side and a "P. M." happy face on the
other. The handle with machined in cap lifter unscrews to reveal the worm. $10-20.

Traveling funnels come complete with a cap lifter,
a corkscrew, and a carrying case. $100-150.

Grippers & Snippers

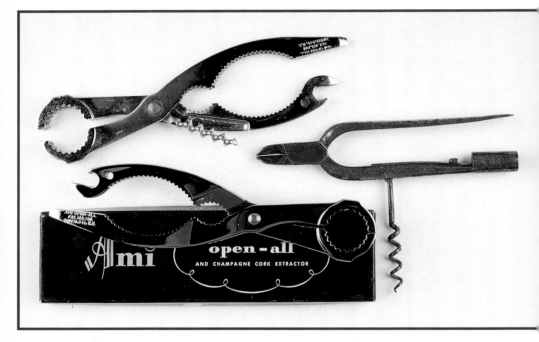

Left top and bottom: 1967 patent by Joseph Amigone of Buffalo, New York, including a corkscrew on a "Gripper Type Cork Extractor." $80-100; Earlier 1951 patent "Ami open-all and champagne cork extractor" without corkscrew. $25-35.
Right: Unmarked steel wire cutter tool with corkscrew. $200-300. Note: A more common version has no corkscrew and is valued at $50-75.

Lazy Tongs

The Lazy Tongs corkscrew is also often referred to as a Concertina, Compound Lever, or even by the well known trade name ZIG ZAG. The United States patent classification for the type of action in this corkscrew is Lazy Tongs. The English patents of Wier (1884) and Armstrong (1902) refer to the mechanism as Lazy-Tongs.

In the lazy tongs corkscrew design, the worm is affixed to the lowest linkage in a series of bars, which add a mechanical advantage to the corkscrew. With the tool compressed, the worm is inserted into the cork until the collar comes to rest on the bottle neck. By pulling on the handle top, the cork is easily removed with little effort.

The "Zig Zag" at *top center* is the most common Lazy Tongs and was produced in many variations. Values range from $30-100. At *top left* is a version without the cap lifters on the levers. $75-100. *Bottom left* is a cheaply made Lazy Tongs marked MADE IN FRANCE. $20-30. At *bottom center* is the "Kis-Ply," which has a wire spring in the circle at top. This is Jean Thomas' 1932 French Patent. $150-200. The unmarked Lazy Tongs at *right* has a cast handle. $80-100.

Top left: Henry Armstrong's 1902 patent marked THE "PULLEZI" and HEELEY'S ORIGINAL PATENT. $150-300.

Bottom left: Wier's 1885 patent corkscrew marked PAT. NOV. 10 1885 "THE RELIABLE." $150-300.

Top right: Wier's 1884 patent marked PATENT WEIR'S PATENT 12804, 25 SEPTEMBER 1884, HEELEY & SONS, MAKERS. $175-250.

Bottom right: French lazy tongs marked DEBOUCHTOUT, BTE S.G.D.G., MARQUE ET MODELE DEPOSES FRANCE ET ETRANGER. Has cap lifters on the bottom link. $150-175.

Metal T-handles

The idea of an all metal corkscrew with shank and worm connected perpendicularly to a fixed handle is one of the simplest forms of a corkscrew. Cheap to produce, impervious to fire, and susceptible to rust, hundreds of variations of these exist. Like their wood handle cousins, many 20th century examples were used for advertising purposes.

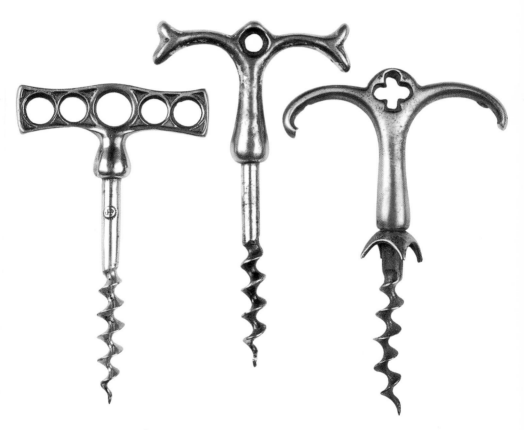

Left to right: Handle with slight two finger grip with mark of Jacques Perille. $100-150; Clawfoot handle with bulbed shank. $100-125; Fancy design with cork gripping teeth. $150-250.

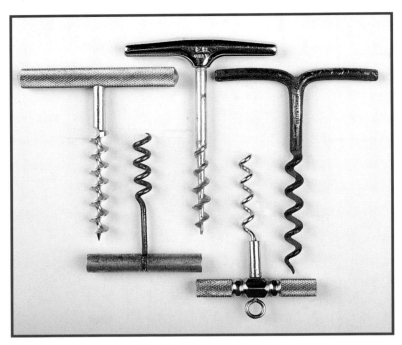

Various simple designs. $10-50.

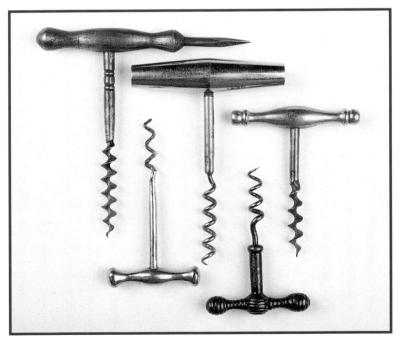

Various designs having a little more detail or weight. $25-75.
The steel handle with wire/ice breaker spike is valued at $50-75.

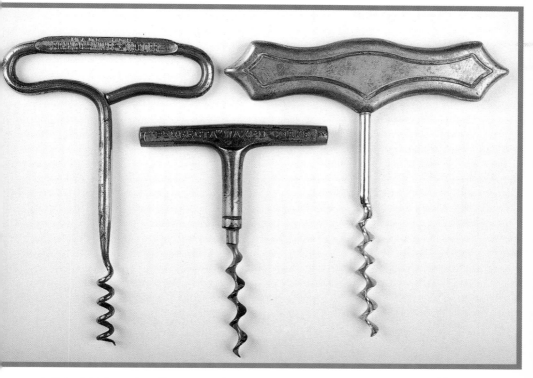

Left to right: Loop handle advertising "Made for Franco's Wines & Liquors." $60-80; Advertising "E. Marwood & Co. Liverpool & Blackburn, 'Perfecta' Waxed Corks." $65-75; Heavy Art Deco handle. $40-60

Mid-Size

Mid-size corkscrews are in the 3" to 4 1/2" overall length range with 2" to 3" handle widths. Most were used for withdrawing small corks from bottles containing liquids other than wine, beer, or liquor. They are seldom found with marks. Horn, bone, and ivory handles are usually French.

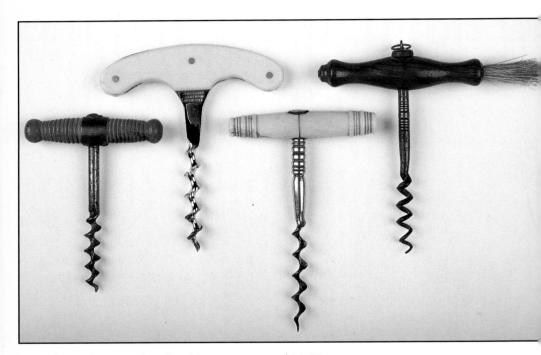

Left to right: Wood handle with narrow worm. $15-25; Celluloid scales on two finger formed steel handle by John Watts, Sheffield, England. $125-150; Turned ivory handle. $125-150; Wood handle T with brush. $50-60.

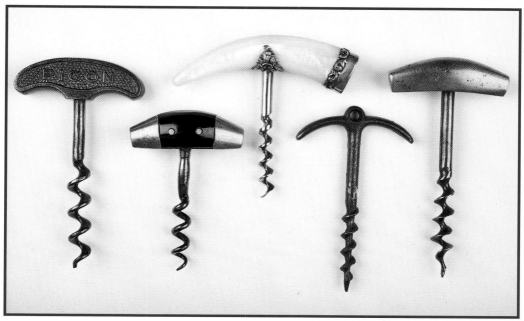

Left to right: Iron handle marked PICON. $50-60; Thin horn scales mounted on solid brass handle. $100-150; Mother-of-pearl with sterling mount. $250-300; Iron for two small fingers. $30-40; Machined brass. $60-70.

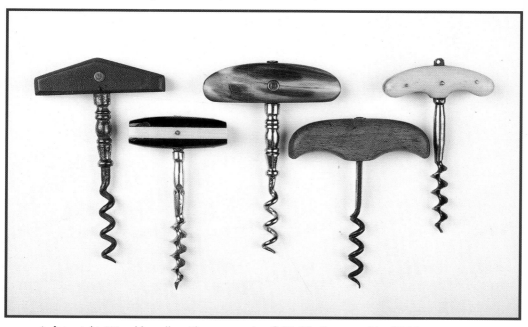

Left to right: Wood handle with green paint. $40-60; Oreo cookie. $100-150; Horn with shaft peened over washer at top *and* secured by pin on side. $100-120; Wood two finger handle with flat part of shank marked FRANCE. $50-60; Celluloid ivory. $50-60.

Miniature

A wide variety of miniature corkscrews have been manufactured. These replicate their parents and were used as perfume corkscrews, charms, and salesman's samples. A 1928 German catalog from Bolte & Anschütz lists a mini T-Handle, a mini frame, and a mini bow as "Flacon-Korkenzieher" (Corkscrews for small bottles).

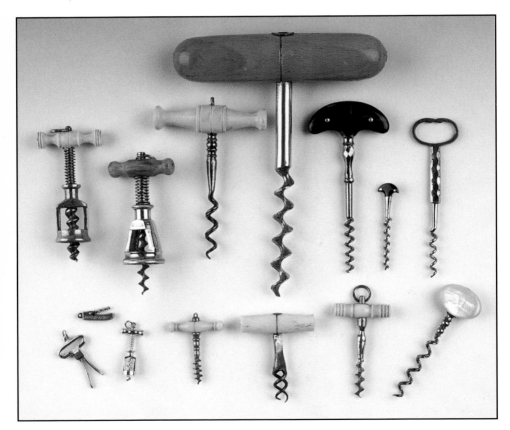

Frame types were made with ivory and bone handles. $100-300.
For size relationship, the small tortoise shell handle is 1 1/2" long, while its "mother" is 3". $75-150.
Charms have been produced in sterling, ivory, and gold. $50-200.
T-handle direct pulls can be found from 1" to 2 3/4" with handles of ivory, bone, brass, celluloid, and plastic. $30-200.

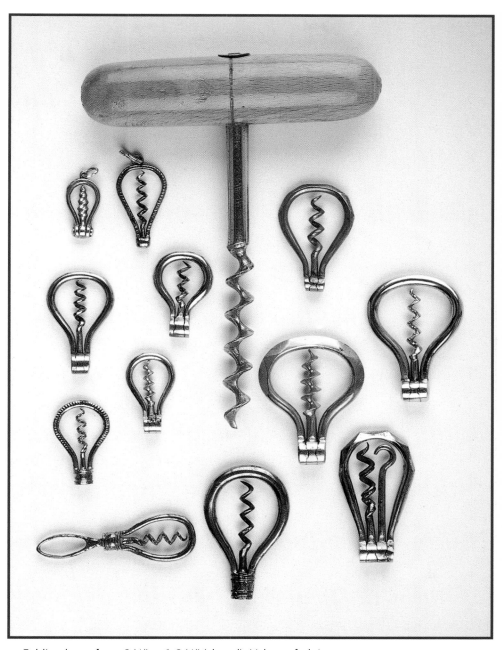

Folding bows from 3/4" to 1 3/4" (closed). Values of plain, unmarked examples with worm only will range from $20-40; Faceted, unmarked examples $40-70; Fancy marked examples $75-100. An extraordinary folding bow is *at lower left*. It has a one piece worm and glove hook rotating in frame. $200-300.

Murphy

The Murphy Company was founded in Boston, Massachusetts, in 1850 and later relocated three times to surrounding communities. Murphy manufactured a wide range of cutlery products including cork-screws, knives, chisels, cigar box openers, cheese testers, burnishing irons, and more. T-Handle Murphy corkscrews will normally be marked on the shank. Frame types are marked on the top of the frame.

Left to right: Dark acorn handle marked MURPHY. $70-100; Murphy patent marked PAT. APR. 23 '01, R. MURPHY on shank. $80-120; Frame with locking handle marked R. MURPHY, BOSTON. $75-100; Acorn handle with frame marked R. MURPHY, BOSTON. $80-100.

Needle

In needle cork lifters, air is pumped manually or gas is injected into the area between the liquid and the cork. A needle with holes near the point is pushed through the cork. The pressure of the air will either break the bottle or, hopefully, push the cork out.

Needle cork lifters can be found at flea markets as "distressed" or "close out" merchandise at prices ranging from $1 to $10. New ones are sold in retail stores and through mail order catalogs. For example, *The Wine Enthusiast* currently offers a black "Corkette" for $14.95.

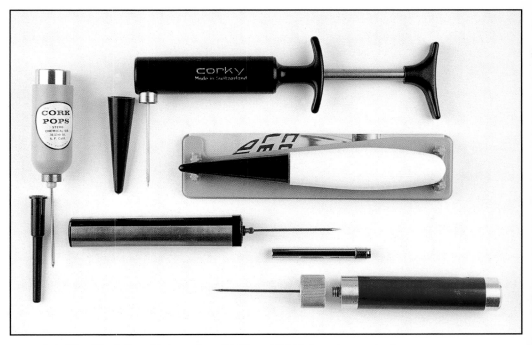

Left: The "Cork Pops" is based on 1963 and 1965 American patents issued to George Federighi. These incorporate a cartridge that, at the push of a button, injects a gas into the bottle to lift the cork.
Right top to bottom: "Corky" from Switzerland. This Swiss patent has a reciprocating pump action; "Corkette" from England; "Cork Lifter" from Germany; The red cork lifter has no name. The needle is inserted through the cork and the handle is moved up and down to supply air. The needle reverses to store in the handle.

Nifty

A corkscrew frequently found at flea markets is the "Nifty" type." Millions were produced for advertising purposes. And by the huge numbers that turn up, those sold as the "Nifty" and marketed as such must have been made in even greater numbers! The "Nifty" was invented in 1916 by Harry L. Vaughan and produced by his Chicago firm. A less common version was patented by Thomas Harding in 1928 and manufactured by the J. L. Sommer Manufacturing Company of Newark, New Jersey. This improved Harding design was a single stamping with worm riveted to it. It was easier, faster, and less expensive to manufacture than the Vaughan type, which was a double stamping folded over the pivoting worm.

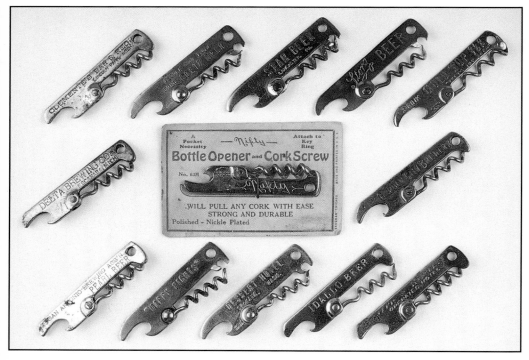

Nifty style corkscrews can be found with a variety of marks, opener, and worm variations and with hundreds of different advertisements. All too often they are advertised, labeled, or promoted as rare, unique, or unusual. If it only says "Nifty," it is worth very little. Values on those with advertising will depend very much on the product advertised and how badly the specialist or collector wants it. Common Nifties advertising "Gallagher and Burton" turn up all the time priced from $1 to $25. A beer advertising collector will pay $10-50 depending upon the obscurity of the brand advertised. A Nifty advertising "Cracker Jack" was run up to $93.79 on an internet auction in an unusual bidding frenzy.

Ornate Frames

Although there are not many different "ornate frame" corkscrews, one or two varieties are certain to add a little pizzazz to any corkscrew collection. Several of the nickel and silver plated Rococo design frames with locking rollover handles have turned up at London auctions in recent years. A brass Satyr with ornamental frame brought over £1000 in a 1997 auction. Another brass figural in the same auction sold for over £3500.

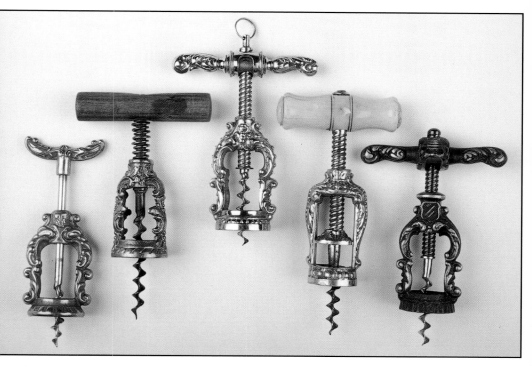

Left to right: Italian brass ornate frames. Modern. $50-60; Ornate cast frame with spring and wood handle. $200-300; Rococo design frame with locking rollover handle. $300-800; Nickel plated brass frame with bone handle and lifting and centering button on the worm. $250-350; Verdigris with gold tone finishes on ornate frame with rollover handle. $80-100.

The two cherubs at the top are picking grapes from a vine and the two at the bottom are holding a cask. In 1976, it brought a record price of £1050 for corkscrews at Christie's London. In a 1985 sale at Sotheby's in London, it sold for a record £4620. Sotheby's described it as a "19th century English style corkscrew." *$Rare.*

Peg & Worm

Worm = the part that is turned into the cork. Peg = a tapered spike that is stored in the center of the worm and removed and inserted into a hole at the top of the worm for use. They come in many shapes and sizes and date back to the late 18th century. They are made of steel and are brass, chrome, nickel, silver, or gold plated. The worms were usually wire or fluted.

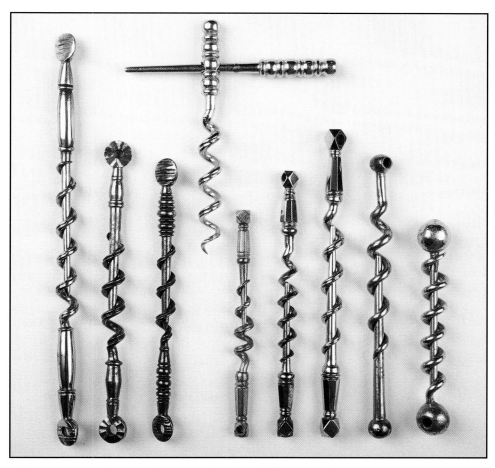

An assortment of peg and worm corkscrews with button ends, faceted ends, and ball ends. Values range from $75 to $200.

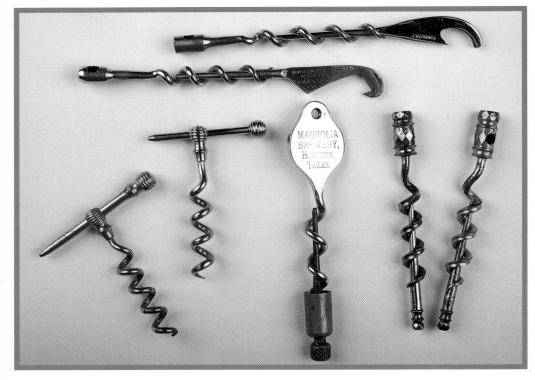

Top two: First marked only PROV. PAT. (Provisional Patent) with the conventional under the lip cap lifter. $80-120; Second has an over-the-top style cap lifter patented by A. W. Flint & Co. in England, France, Germany, and the United States in the 1920s. $100-150.

At *left* is a matched set of left and right hand pegs and worms. $200-250/set. On the *right* are brass and nickel plated pegs and worms with faceted ends and unusually wide fluted worms. $125-150.

The peg and worm in the *center* is Edwin Walker's 1898 American patent in which the peg securely threads into the top of the handle, which was an ideal place for advertising. This one is for "Magnolia Brewery, Houston, Texas." Most of these were produced with a left-hand worm. $150-250.

Perfume

Why would a lady have a corkscrew in an implement set in her dressing or sitting room? She needed it to open perfumes, ink bottles, and medicines.

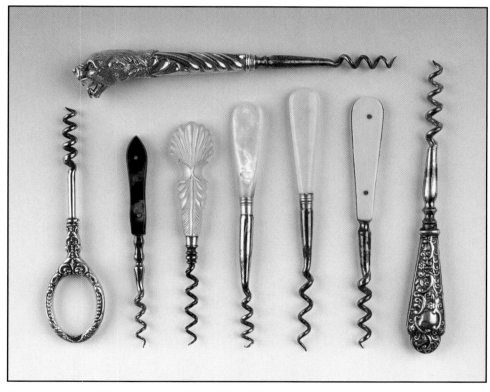

Top: A tiger head (Birmingham 1896). $300-400.
Left: A finger loop shown in a 1900 catalog of Daniel Low & Co. of Salem, Massachusetts. $125-150.
The *rest* have various handle types - tortoise shell, mother-of-pearl, ivory, bone, and silver. There are many different handle designs and corkscrew lengths. Most of these came from dressing table sets that might have included thimbles, button hooks, stilettos, needle cases, penknives, crochet hooks, scissors, bodkins, and/or tweezers. $20-150.

Picnic

A picnic corkscrew has a worm with a short shaft and a ring in the top. The worm is protected by a sheath, which can be inserted into the ring at the top to form the handle. It is a very convenient stowaway corkscrew for the picnic basket.

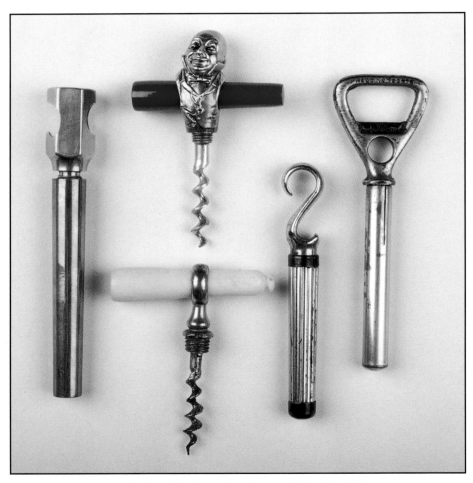

Left: Unmarked brass hex head with machined in cap lifter. $25-35.
Second Column: Pickwick figure with red bakelite sheath. $150-200; Corkscrew with white celluloid sheath. $60-80.
Next: Knud Knudsen's 1939 American patent. $40-60.
Right: A 1924 English registered design with cap lifter above sheath insertion hole. $80-100.

The sheaths of picnic corkscrews can be found in steel, brass, nickel plated brass, pewter, silver, and wood. Most are not marked and are valued at $100-200. Marked picnics can add $50-100 to the value. Wood sheath examples (*left and right*) are rare. $200-300.

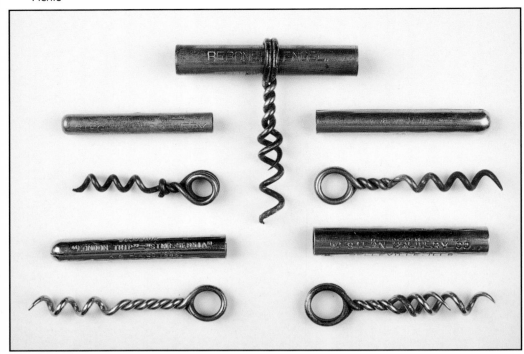

Various advertising on sheaths encasing wire worms. $50-100.

A group of French boxwood picnic corkscrews. The sheaths are threaded for secure storage of the worm. They can be found with many different advertisements for well known modern companies and have values ranging from $1-6. The picnic at the *top* is a bit unusual in design and difficult to find. This one is a souvenir of Liechtenstein. $20-30. At *left* is a hand painted example featuring champagne bottle, top hat, glass, and party favors. $20-25.

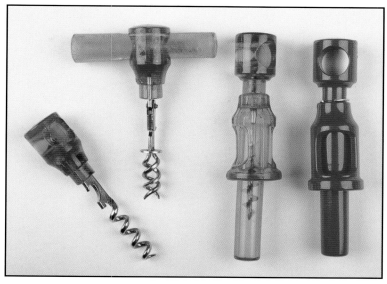

Left to right: Italian green picnic with cap lifter in shank. $4-5:
Double helix picnic with folding cap lifter. $6-8; Clear orange
with frame marked MADE IN ITALY. The addition of the self
pulling frame makes this picnic a much more practical tool.
$5-6; Red sheath with frame marked PICNIC TIME. $8-10.

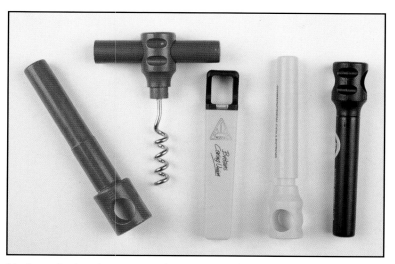

Modern plastic advertising corkscrews can often be found
in hotel rooms (free!) or in liquor stores for very little cost.
Souvenir shop examples with place names vary from $1-4.
In housewares departments, prices are less than $2. Older
out-of-business advertisers are valued at $1-4.

Plastic

Corkscrews have been manufactured using man made materials for well over a century. Goodyear's 1851 patent dealt with hard rubber. Hard rubber was used in the production of some roundlets. Celluloid was developed in 1856. In 1909, Bakelite appeared and corkscrews were produced using that material. In a 1946 catalog, the Williamson Company advertises corkscrews with red and green catalin sheaths and handles.

Plastics are any synthetic organic material molded under heat and pressure. If you already own celluloid, bakelite, or catalin corkscrews, you have "plastic" corkscrews. They add bright colors to your collection. You can't avoid them; they are everywhere. In the late 1960s, the plastics revolution in corkscrews began to move forward by leaps and bounds. In 30 years, plastic corkscrews in hundreds of sizes, shapes, and colors have been produced.

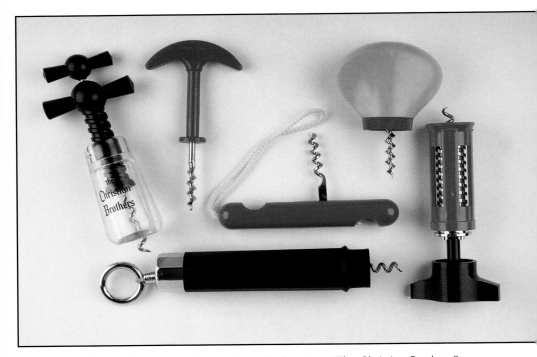

Left to right: Double action with clear barrel advertising "The Christian Brothers" wines. $20-25; Red two finger pull with "button" from Hong Kong. $2-3; Red folder from Hong Kong. The cap lifter, corkscrew, *and* nylon hanging rope are sandwiched between two molded halves. $4-5; A mid-1980s full grip corkscrew invented by Gunther Pracht in Germany. By continuously turning the handle, the cork is extracted with little effort. Produced in Germany and Spain. $5-10; The "Grand Prix" from Crossbow Inc., Cincinnati, Ohio. $10-15.
Bottom: A telescope marked KARIBA. A 1983 patent covered the rope and pulley mechanics of this corkscrew and a 1990 patent was for the design. $15-20.

Pocket Folders

Folding corkscrews were designed primarily to be kept in one's vest pocket or purse. As cork extractors, most are not very practical. The worm folds to a point on its metal host to protect the owner from being stabbed and to prevent the device from poking holes in one's pocket or purse. Many were used for advertising purposes. Although convenient, most would not easily remove a stubborn cork.

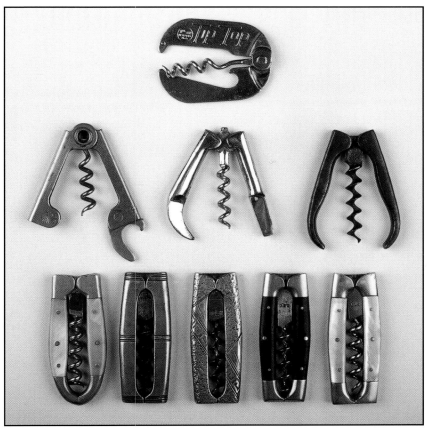

Top: The "Tip Top" by Williamson of Newark, New Jersey. $40-60. Those found with advertising value $75-80.
Middle row left to right: The "Chief" depicting an Indian head with headdress. $40-50; German folder with carriage key and foil cutter. $100-150; A simple unmarked German folder. $75-100.
Bottom row left to right: Mother-of-pearl handles marked GERMANY. $350-450; Nickel silver handles marked WILSON CO. $175-200; Fancy nickel silver handles marked WILSON CO. $250-300; Wood grain handles and mother-of-pearl handles marked G & S (for Graef & Schmidt) on one side of the shank and the Henckel's Twin trademark on the other. Graef & Schmidt were the New York City based importers of Henckel's Twin Brand cutlery at the turn of the century. $250-325.

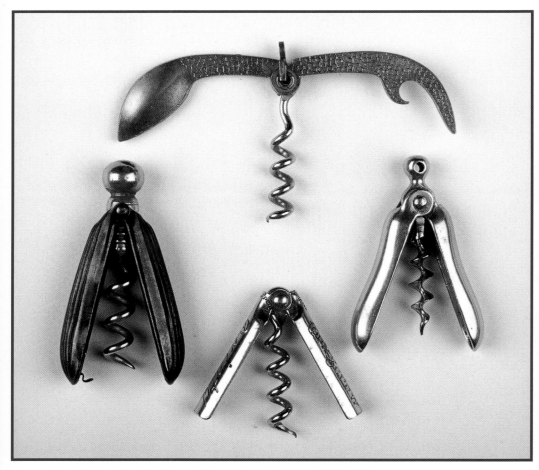

Top: "Turkey Foot" with cap lifter and small spoon. $125-150.
Bottom left to right: "Clam Shell" with spring clip on the
bottom to secure the sides when not in use. $200-300; The
"Dainty" by Vaughan, Chicago, Illinois. The Dainty was also
used as an advertising giveaway. $125-150; "Pea Pod" by
Perille in Paris. $200-300.

Top: Marked "SO-EZY" MADE IN U.S.A. PAT. PEND. $40-50.
Bottom left to right: Cap lifter with a pin holding the worm between
two shoulders advertising "Suze Aperitif." $30-40; From Vaughan,
Chicago, a bottle shape cap lifter with worm riveted to the backside, ready to swivel out for cork removal. Advertising on the other
side is "Broadway Sports Palace, Management, Schork & Schaffer."
$40-50; "Compliments of Bishop's Liquor Store, 217 S. Akard,
Phone 2-8523." $80-100; Two "Over-the-top" cap lifters patented
by Harry Vaughan in Chicago in 1924. $25-50.

Left side top to bottom: Thomas Harding's 1928 American patent for his version of the Nifty cap lifter/corkscrew. This one is quite unusual in that it has a three inch rule on one side and a file on the other. $60-80; A German corkscrew fashioned in the Nifty style has an added can opener in the military P-38 style. $75-100; A heavier German made piece advertising "Melchers Distilleries Limited, St. Lawrence Bourbon Whiskey." $80-90; An English combination cap lifter, can opener, and corkscrew folder. $50-75.

Middle top to bottom: Long arm folder with cap lifter for a full grip. $75-100; Harry Chippendale's 1910 American Patent for the addition of a cigar cutter. $800-1000.

Right side top to bottom: Robert McLean's 1926 American patent for a combination corkscrew, cigar box opener, and bottle opener. $200-300; Augustus Stephens 1901 Design Patent for a cap lifter which is frequently found with brewery advertising. It is unusual to see this design with a corkscrew added. $75-85; A pointing hand is a spinner used at a bar to determine who pays. $100-125; A German combination cap lifter, can opener, and corkscrew folder. $50-75.

Prong Pullers & Retrievers

A very common advertising giveaway today is a cork puller with two prongs sometimes referred to as a "screwless extractor." The advertising is usually on a plastic case and they can be found with the names of a host of wineries. The prong puller is not a recent invention! They have been around since the 19th century.

Do they work? With a little practice, you will be surprised at how easily you can extract a cork without doing damage to it. Simply start sliding the longer of the prongs down one side of the cork. Then, using a rocking motion, work both down as far as you can. Turn the handle to break the seal between the cork and the bottle and then lift.

Top row left to right: In 1879 and 1892, Lucian Mumford's American patents were granted for a cork puller called the "Magic Cork Extractor." $500-700; Rare version of Mumford patent with flat retainer above prongs. $900-1100; Modern cork puller marked GOURMET. $20-25.
Bottom row left to right: Silver handle example of Machil Converse's 1899 American patent. $300-400; Common wood handle Converse prong puller with nickel plated brass sheath. $25-35; A cylindrical wood case protects the equal length rounded end prongs. The puller is from Argentina and the base is marked IN VINO VERITAS. $100-150.

Left to right: A prong puller with cap lifter that swivels out from inside the handle. Marked FOR CROWN CORKS, W.U.F. IDEAL CORKPULLER, BRITISH MADE. $90-100; Vaughan's (Chicago) "Quick and Easy Cork Puller and Bottle Opener." $30-50; A French puller marked SAN BRI B^TE S.G.D.G. A spare set of prongs is stored in the sheath. $125-150.

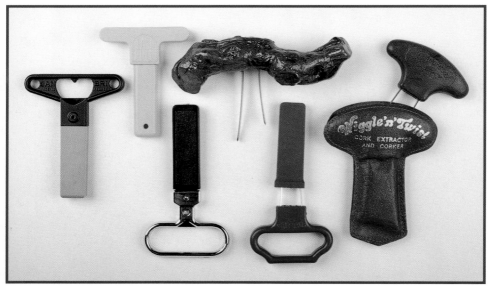

Left to right: Black metal puller marked SAN BRI with plastic sheath. $30-40; English puller marked EASI PULL made by the Easi-Pull Co. Hove, Sussex. $15-20; Chrome Italian puller with black plastic sheath. $8-10; Grapevine roots with worm are quite common - here is a rare genuine example with prongs. $60-80; Burgundy plastic puller marked TWISTUP. $8-10; Wiggle 'n Twist Cork Extractor and Corker with leather case. A 1979 English patent. $35-40.

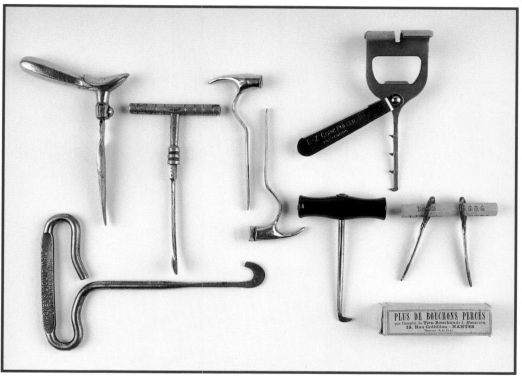

Top row left to right: A French single blade cork lifter marked B^{IE} S.G.D.G. $400-500; An 1873 French patent by Eugene Mestre, the puller is pushed down between the cork and the bottle. When the hook is below the cork, it can be turned to grab the cork and pull it up. $500-700; An 1886 French Patent by Dugert and Lafittau. The two prongs are stored by putting the prong tips into the slot in the handle of the opposing piece. $800-1000; The "E-Z Cork Puller" has a toothed shaft with folding cover. $65-75.

Bottom row left to right: American made hooked cork lifter with advertising for Wacker's Liquid Malt. $125-150; Benjamin Greely's 1888 American Patent. As the hook is inserted into the cork, a groove in the shaft allows air to escape. When the hook is below the cork, it is turned and the cork can be "lifted" out. $300-350; A 1904 French patented puller comprising a wood dowel and two prongs. $25-35.

Rack & Pinion

In a rack and pinion corkscrew, the pinion meshes with a rack with teeth to lift a cork from a bottle. The collar is placed over the bottle neck and the worm is turned into the cork by turning the top handle. The side handle turns the pinion to engage the rack. These are also referred to as "Sidewinders."

Left to right: "Four poster" King's Screw with bone top handle. $800-1200; Lund Bottle Grips corkscrew. *$Rare;* A barrel form rack and pinion with patent plate marked DOWLER. $800-$1400; Marked below handle LUND'S PATENT RACK and marked on frame sides LUND MAKER CORNHILL AND FLEET ST. LONDON. $350-400; Unmarked. $150-200.

Roundlets

Roundlets originated in the 18th century with the hinged barrel type containing a double hinged worm. Later versions had cases that either unscrewed or pulled apart with the worm stored in one end. One side is removed, the worm is pulled out and turned perpendicular to the case, then the empty side is threaded or pushed back on to form the handle. A third type is the roundlet that contains several loose tools with one or two slots in their shafts to mate with one or two slots in the case. Lighters, hammers, rasps, spoons, cap lifters, and whistles have also been attached in various ways. Roundlets can be found in brass, steel, wood, gold, silver, celluloid, rubber, and plastic. The roundlet specialist can build a rather extensive collection by looking at the great number of variations in design, size, and material.

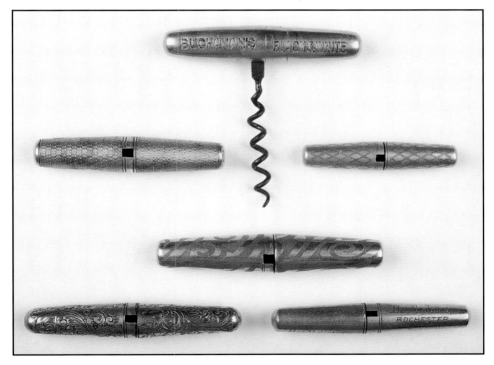

Finely machined and engraved nickel plated roundlets with threaded cases including two with advertising. $150-250.

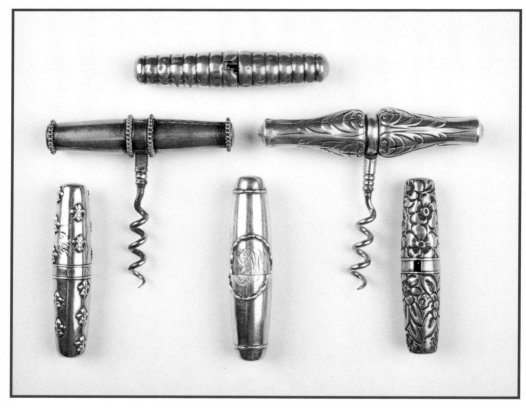

A group of ornate Sterling roundlets with threaded cases. Marks including "L" trademark of La Pierre (New York and Connecticut), Gorham trademark (Providence, Rhode Island), Tiffany & Co. (New York, New York), and H & H (Providence). $200-600.

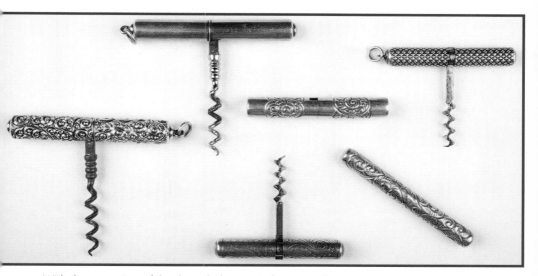

With the exception of the threaded case sterling roundlet in the center, all of these slide apart to expose the worm and slide back together to form the handle. $150-300.

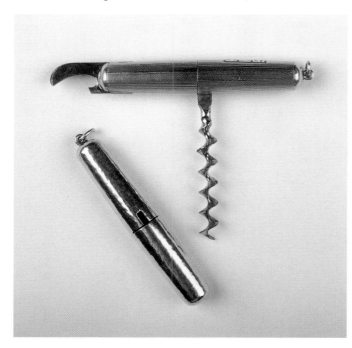

Top: Gold roundlet with worm shank marked GERMANY. Cap lifter at end. Marked 14K and engraved with initials "S M H." $800-1000. *Bottom:* English 18ct hallmarked for Chester 1899. $1200-1500.

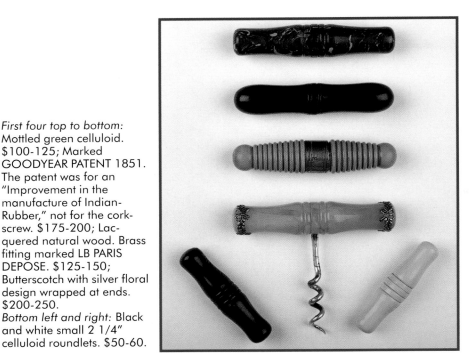

First four top to bottom: Mottled green celluloid. $100-125; Marked GOODYEAR PATENT 1851. The patent was for an "Improvement in the manufacture of Indian-Rubber," not for the cork-screw. $175-200; Lac-quered natural wood. Brass fitting marked LB PARIS DEPOSE. $125-150; Butterscotch with silver floral design wrapped at ends. $200-250.
Bottom left and right: Black and white small 2 1/4" celluloid roundlets. $50-60.

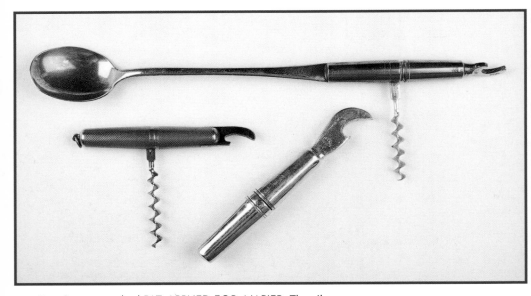

Top: Spoon marked PAT. APPLIED FOR, NAPIER. The silver-smith married the spoon with a German roundlet. $200-250.
Bottom left and right: Nicely machined German roundlet with cap lifter. $125-150; Marked ASPREY LONDON and R^D N^O 691160 (1922 English Registered Design). $400-500.

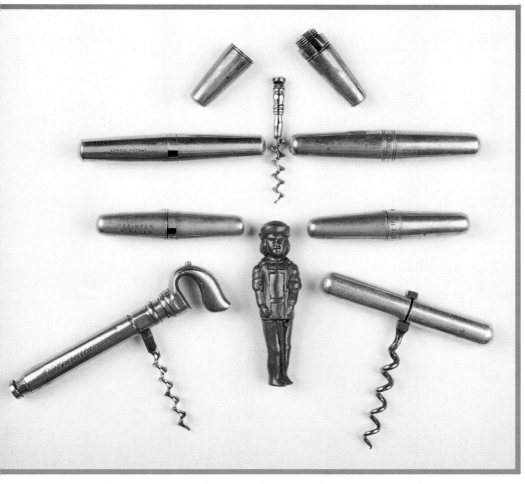

Top: Benoit Thinet's 1873 French patent. The worm is loose in the case. $40-50.
Second row left and right: 1855 English patent marked LUND'S PATENT
SPHERICAL JOINT LONDON. $125-150; Middle band marked with the famous
maker FARROW & JACKSON. $100-125.
Third row left and right: Marked VERINDER S^T PAULS. $75-100; An 1873
English Registered design by George Wright and Charles Bailey marked with
registration date. $60-80.
Bottom row left to right: Figural roundlet advertising "Boyer Hammer, Consoli-
dated Pneumatic Tool C^O L$^{D.}$" $250-300; Christopher Columbus figure marked
COLUMBUS SCREW 1492 CHICAGO 1892. $500-600; A 1903 English patent
by S. R. G. Vaughan marked G. F. HIPKINS & SON BIRMINGHAM PATENTED,
PIC-NIC PATENT. $200-250.

Sardine Keys

A combination tool with a cork-screw *and* a sardine tin key? One would think this would be an unlikely contrivance and, if found, a unique one. Although these are not ordinarily found, they are by no means unique.

Top: A sardine can opener/corkscrew with a folding fork for eating the sardines once the lid is opened. $150-200.
Left two: Combination tool marked DEPOSE FRANCE. $40-50; Marked PATENTE NO. 27116 with a BOJ trademark (a trademark of B. Olanta y Juaristi in Spain). $30-40.
Right two: A tool that can cut, remove a cork, open a tin can, remove a bottle cap, crack a nut, cut wire, cut cigars, remove cigar box lid nails, punch leather, drive screws, file metal, and even open a sardine can. $250-350; A "waiter's friend" complete with sardine key. The "Yatout" by Perille of Paris. $400-500.

Scissors

The scissors style corkscrew/ champagne wire cutter was an 1893 German design registration by Thill and Küll, cutlery manufacturers in Solingen, Germany. In their design, the arms folded out to form the handle for the protected worm. In France, the scissors style corkscrew often included a cigar tip cutter.

Left to right: Scissors style corkscrew/wire cutter marked G. M. S. NO. 10985 and GERMANY. $300-350; A French scissors style with cigar tip cutter and wire cutter. Advertising for "Gerard de Reconde." $500-600; A rare scissors style corkscrew with ornate design on German silver handles. $800-1000.

Spoons

Cocktail spoons with corkscrews have been found with coast to coast advertising. Advertisers include hotels, breweries, distilleries, retail stores, special events, museums, laundries, and funeral homes. Values are apt to be driven up by collectors of advertising from particular businesses or of local interest material.

Spoons with folding corkscrew handles are good reminders that the corkscrew was not simply used for wine, beer, or spirits. They were used to remove corks from medicine bottles and then take a dose of the medicine. The combination was a late 19th century invention.

Left to right: A spoon with two folds with the trademark of silversmiths Currier & Roby of New York City. $300-400; An advertising spoon: "Tabloids of Compressed Drugs, Hazeline Cream, Keppler Extract Essence of Malt, Keppler Solution of Cod Liver Oil, Digestive, Demulgent, Strengthening, Hazeline Beer & Iron Wine." $150-175; A tablespoon with corkscrew. Sterling with a gold wash in the bowl and a gold plated worm. $300-350.

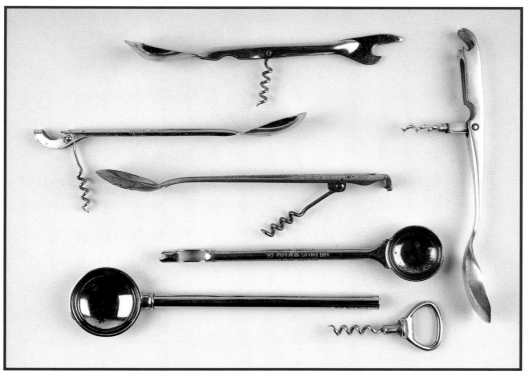

The five spoons on the *left* can be found with a wide variety of advertisements and marks. Values range from $10-40. The spoon on the *right* is a silverplated 1932 American patent by Walker and Orr. So the spoon handle can be gripped properly, this sensible invention has the worm folding out of the center instead of the end of the spoon. $100-125.

Silver

Silver corkscrews have been produced for a couple of hundred years. They are sought after not only by the corkscrew collector, but by decorators who want an accent for the dining room table or the owner of a wine cellar who wants a prize for his cellar. Prices on silver and other precious metal corkscrews continue to escalate as the competition for them grows.

Cap lifters with ornate silver handles are often seen at antiques shows and in antiques shops. Prices will range from $25-50. But when one finds a corkscrew hiding in that silver handle, the price jumps to $75-125.

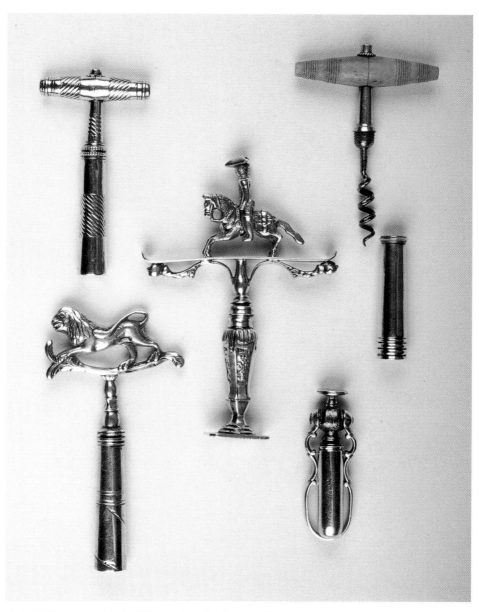

Late 18th century/early 19th century English and Dutch pocket corkscrews with silver fittings and sheaths. Various handles of ivory, silver, and mother-of-pearl. $900-1500.

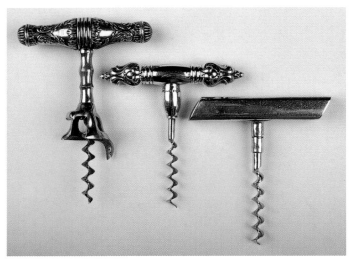

Left to right: A Walker 1900 American patent bell cap with trademark of Providence, Rhode Island silversmiths Foster & Bailey. $200-300; A direct pull with trademark of Watrous Manufacturing Company of Meriden, Connecticut. $200-300; A simple Art Deco style handle by John Hasselbring of Brooklyn, New York. $200-250.

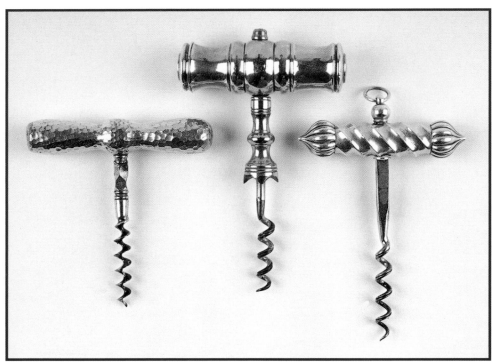

Left to right: Peanut shaped handle ends. $400-500; Corkscrew with cork grips at the bottom of the shank. 1900 Birmingham, England, hallmark. $800-1000. English silver corkscrew with onion fluted caps, square shank, and fluted worm. 1890 Birmingham hallmark. $500-600.

Single Levers

Like the double lever corkscrew, the single lever is rather simple and easy to use. Instead of having two arms to raise the cork, the user has a single arm leverage. The most common type of single lever corkscrews is the "Waiter's Friend." Here are some of the most difficult to find single levers.

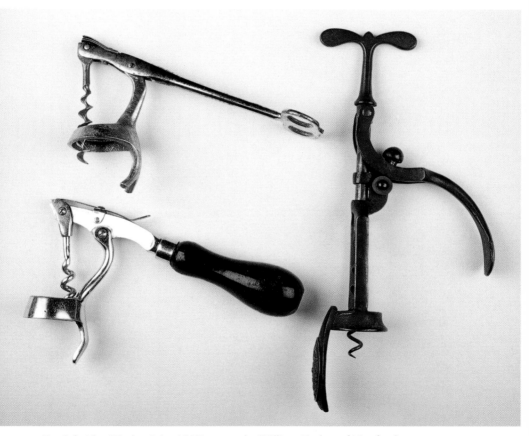

Top left: The "Tucker." An 1878 patent by William Tucker of Hartford, Connecticut. In 1882, "Tuckers" were offered for sale in a Russell & Erwin hardware catalog at $10 per dozen. Today's value: $1800-3000 each.
Bottom left: The "Sperry." An 1878 patent by Alfred Sperry of Wallingford, Connecticut. It was offered for sale in an 1881 catalog from Simmons Hardware of St. Louis, Missouri, for $1.25! Today's value: $2500-3500.
Right: The "Royal Club" is one of the most sought after single levers. It was patented in England in 1864 by Charles Hull. $2500-4500.

A number of English patents were issued in the 19th century for a lever handle that would lift a cork by means of a rather simple worm screwed into the cork separately: Lund and Hipkins, 1854; Wolverson, 1873; and Goodall, 1885 and 1889. In the 1980s, these turned up frequently for sale at London markets for £10-30. Today's value: $100-250.

Slide Out

In 1892, Edmund Jansen in Germany received a patent (#6145) for a corkscrew that slides out of a channel formed by folding sheet metal into a rectangle. One end and half of the underside are left open for the sliding mechanism. A backspring is located in the top of the handle and attached to it is a worm with sliding mechanism. The worm slides out the end and is turned perpendicular to the handle locking with the backspring. Sixty years later (1952), Albert Andrews of Fort Collins, Colorado, was granted an American patent for a "Resilient casing with slidable tool." His invention was essentially the same idea as the Jansen invention.

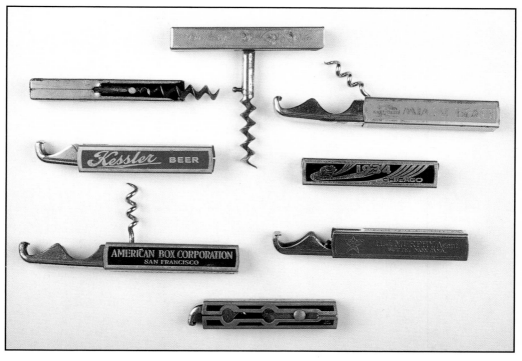

Top center and top left: German and French versions of the Jansen patent. $150-250.
The rest: A colorful assortment of corkscrews from the Electro-Chemical Engraving Co., Inc., 100 Brook Ave., New York. A variety of advertisements can be found. $75-125.

Smokers' Tools

In the hunt for smoker's tools, the corkscrew collector will find stiff competition for his heart's desire. The interest in smoking collectibles (tobacciana) has been fueled by a number of books on the subject. Books have been published on cigar cutters, lighters, chewing tobacco tin tags, camel cigarettes, and smoking collectibles in general. The interests range from worn out old cigarette packs to cigar store Indians. The smoking collector's search includes ashtrays, cigar box openers and cutters, lighters, matchsafes, pipe prickers and tampers, snuff boxes, and tobacco advertising. All of these have been found in combination with corkscrews.

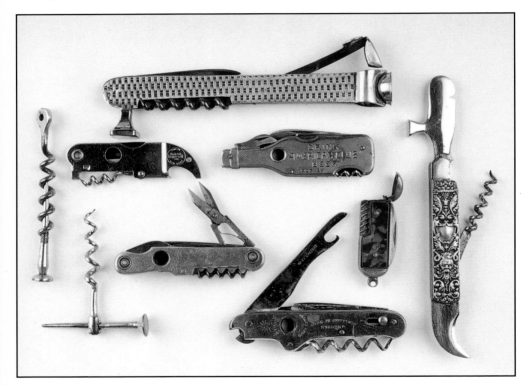

Top and right: In addition to the worm, combination tools may have knives, cigar clippers, tampers, cigar box openers, and/or nail removers. Handles include very plain, monogrammed, intricately decorated, and figural. Lengths of these range from 5 1/2" to 6 1/2". $100-300.
Left and bottom left: "Peg and worm" corkscrews with pipe tampers. $100-200.
Second row: The "Pal, Four in One" uses a razor blade to cut the cigar tip. $75-100; Bottle shape from Griffon Cutlery. $150-200.
Third row: Knife with spring loaded master blade cutting cigar tip in hole. $100-250; English 1892 patent by John Watts. A sliding pin secures a blade which is the pivoting arm of a wire cutter. $75-125; A match safe with match striker. The worm and the knife are not real. $200-250.

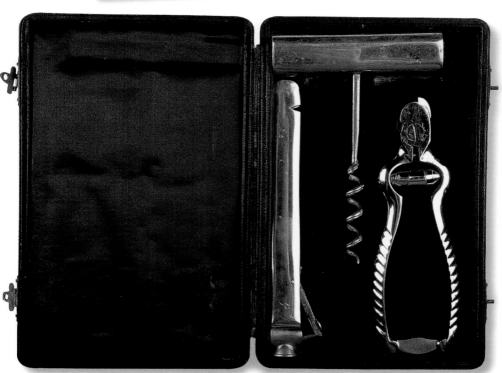

Gentleman's tool set in a fitted case consisting
of combination cigar box opener and cigar
clipper, corkscrew, and wire nippers. $150-200.

Springs

By incorporating a spring in a corkscrew design, the handle is given more pulling power. After the worm is turned into the cork far enough for the frame to come in contact with the bottle neck, the spring begins to exert force against the handle as the user continues to turn the corkscrew. This action causes the cork to be lifted from the bottle.

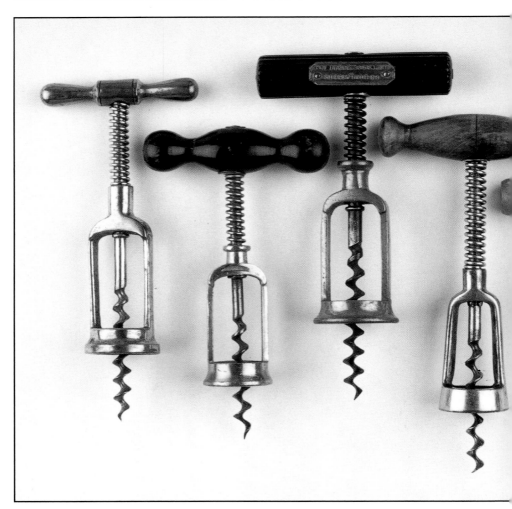

Left to right: All steel unmarked. $60-100; "Hercules." $20-30; Dunisch & Schöler's 1883 German patent. The brass plate has advertising. $100-150; Tapered frame. $40-60; Triangular bell. $30-50.

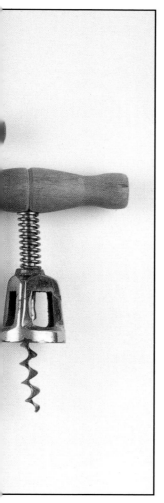

Left: Richard Recknagel's 1899 German patent. The mechanism above the spring has a slot with a diagonal guide and lock that slides up and down over a pin through the shank. $250-300.
Right: A cotter pin in the shank above the worm is an impractical design as there is no way to move the spring barrel out of the way to remove the cork from the worm. $80-100.

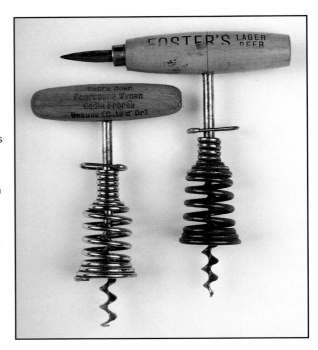

German spring barrels with "paper clip" stop, an 1895 patent by W. Sommers. The oval paper clip has a pin in the center that is inserted in a hole in the shank to stop the spring when removing the cork from the bottle. To remove the cork from the worm, pull the pin out, raise the clip and spring barrel, and unscrew the cork. $90-120.

Left: Dunisch & Schöler's 1883 German patent with an American Walker handle with advertising. $100-150.
Right: A Walker handle with advertising. Instead of the usual cotter pin above the bell, a spring assists the self-pulling bell in removing the cork. $50-60.

Stoppers & Toppers

We often see wood carvings resting atop a cork that is used to reseal a bottle. There are also some very delicate porcelain stoppers and a number of silver, gold, and pewter.

Stoppers and toppers with corkscrews are much more difficult to find and it never hurts to give an unusual stopper a twist to see if there is a worm in the cork.

Top row left to right: Henry Zeilin's 1882 American patent for a "Dose Cup Bottle Stopper." $200-250; A fleur-de-lis topper by Codding Bro. & Heilborn of North Attleboro, Massachusetts (1879-1918). $125-150; A silver dose cup/corkscrew by S. Cottle Co. of New York City (1865-1920). $200-300.
Bottom row left to right: Fox head marked W 10 E. $150-200; Hat style topper marked A. KRUPP BERNDORF with a standing bear trademark. Austria c.1910. $80-100; Bell shape with worm inside by La Pierre Mfg. Co. of New York and New Jersey. $100-150.

Thomason

One of the most important inventions of the 19th century was Sir Edward Thomason's 1802 English patent. His invention allowed the user to remove a cork in one continuous motion. He produced his corkscrews in Birmingham and was one of the first major producers of corkscrews. His mechanism was produced by several manufacturers well into the 20th century.

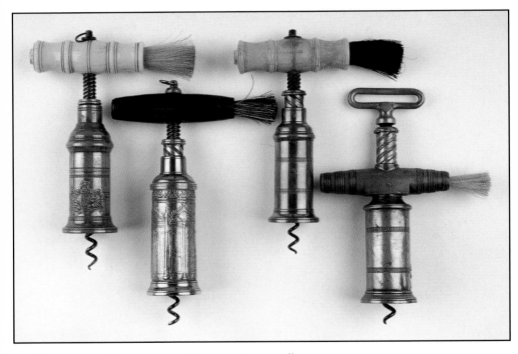

Thomason corkscrews seem to be cropping up all over the place. Recent sales at Christie's in London have seen quite a few of them come under the auction hammer. The *first* and *third* are the most frequently seen. $500-800. The *second* is a rare Thomason barrel depicting Gothic windows. $1500-2000. On the *right* is a Thomason Variant. $750-1500.

Tools

Hammers, picks, wrenches, screwdrivers, hatchets, pliers, glass cutters, and nuts and bolts have all been used in combination corkscrew designs. The reason for the hammer was not as a tool for the carpentry trade, rather as a tool for breaking ice. Wrenches, on the other hand, were, indeed, designed for turning bolts, and a multi-tool with pliers is for gripping or squeezing that which needs to be gripped or squeezed. A close examination of the contents of an old tool box or fisherman's tackle box may very well reward the collector with one of these tools.

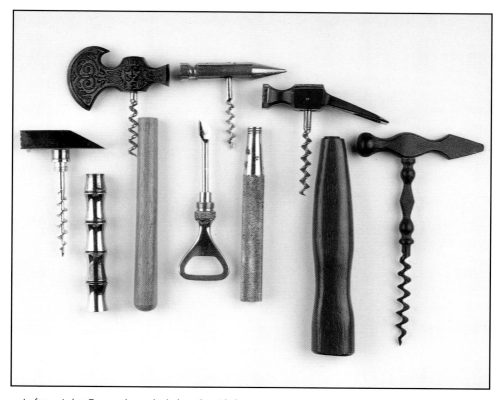

Left to right: Fancy threaded sheath with hammer tag marked SILVER PLATED. $50-75; Hatchet with hammer head, cap lifter, and wood sheath. $30-40; German hammer in three pieces: Sheath rasp handle, cap lifter with unusual end tool, and hammer head with worm. $60-70; Hammer with wood friction fit sheath. $20-30. An early unmarked steel hammer with chopper. $60-70.

Top: Nathan Jenkins' 1930 American Patent for his "15 Tools in One." $150-200.
Second: A French tool including wrench, master knife blade, corkscrew, leather punch, and a blade consisting of cap lifter, ruler, and wire cutter. $200-300.
Bottom left: Erik Nylin's 1909 American patent has these tools: corkscrew, can opener, pipe wrench, tack lifter, hammer, scissors sharpener, knife sharpener, wire stripper, tongs, nut cracker, wrench holes, and file. $500-700.
Bottom right: Italian double nut and bolt. The bottom bolt unthreads to reveal the worm and the top, the cap lifter. $30-40.

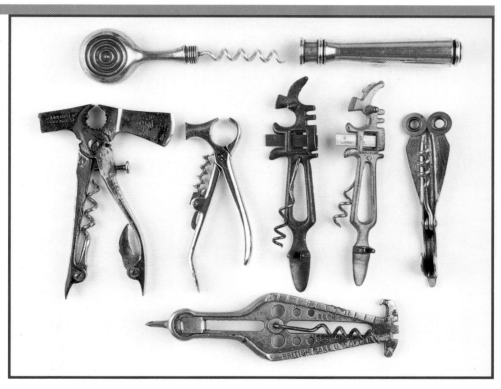

Top: The "Drink Master" by Metal Specialties, Inc., Philadelphia, Pennsylvania, is a bottle opener, an ice breaker, a drink muddler for crushing fruit, and a corkscrew. $40-50.

Middle left to right: 1899 German design registration by Julius Bader. $800-1000; Forged steel multi-tool. $1200-1400; Two tools with an odd combination of a glass cutter and a corkscrew. Tools such as this were patented by Monce (1869), Barrett (1873), Brooks (1874), Woodward (1875), and Adams (1880). $5-20; "The Wizard Knife Sharpener" sharpens knives, lifts lids and bottle caps, and removes corks. $75-100.

Bottom: English 1922 design "Utility" combination tool includes tin opener, corkscrew, bottle cap lifter, bottle stopper wrench, measure, hammer, paper pattern and stencil cutter, coin tester, glass breaker, and, finally, the glass cutter. $65-75.

Above: *Top:* Wood cased tool kit. The corkscrew and other accessories are affixed to the chuck on the end. $200-300.
Bottom: The "Sportsman's Pal" (with leather case) advertised as having 12 uses: "Scaler, Degorger, Gripper, Knife, Scorer, Cutters, Pincers, Splitter, Hone, Screwdriver, Bottle Opener, and Corkscrew." Also found marked FISHERMAN'S FRIEND. $60-75.

Right: A tool set in which all tools (except the pliers) will fit into the end or the side of the wood scale handle. Tool sets have been seen with between six and twenty-one pieces. $100-200.

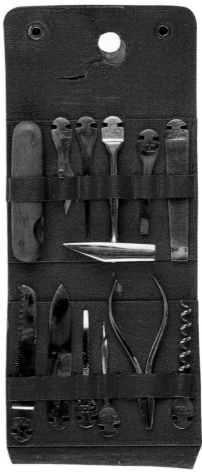

Tusk, Bone & Horn

Tusks, horns, antlers, and bones are articles "found in nature" that are perfect for use as handles or sheaths for corkscrews. Some artists' fine carvings can be found on the very finest of these corkscrews.

Other artifacts were simply shaped into a handle and polished. Some had silver decorative fittings added to the ends and others were hollowed out to serve as the sheaths for worms.

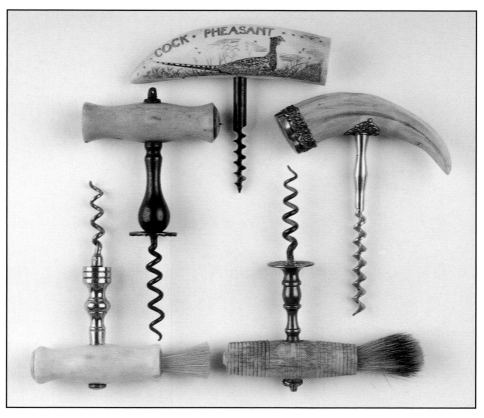

Top: Recent scrimshaw with "Cock Pheasant" on one side and "Red Fox" on the other. $75-100.

Second row left and right: Ivory handle with bulbous shank and gripper button. $125-250; Tusk handles come in many sizes and shapes. Some are fitted with a silver cap on one end and some with caps on both ends. Some caps are plain, while others are ornate. $50-300.

Bottom row left and right: Bone and ivory handles can be found with or without brushes, with shanks from plain and simple to fancy turnings, and with buttons or bells. $50-300.

Top row left to right: John Hasselbring's 1906 American Design Patent for a bottle opener with a "Baltimore Loop Seal" (stopper) remover at the top. The worm is fitted inside a male thread at the bottom and threaded into the silver mount. $75-125; Stag handle with foil cutter. $30-50; Polished ivory with silver mount and simple vine design carved into each side. $200-300; Polished goat horn. $30-50.
Bottom row left to right: English with pressed in 1930-1931 hallmark silver end cap. $60-75; Simple unmarked direct pull with stag handle. $10-30; 4" stag handle with silver mounts on both ends. $25-50.

Unique

In 1917, Wilson Brady was granted a patent for his unique cork remover. The cork remover was supplied in a box that told this story: "Manufactured Only by the Unique Necessites [*sic*] Corporation, 316 St. Paul St., Baltimore, Md., Don't Pull The 'U-Neek' (Trade Mark) Full Directions Inside Pat. Jan. 23, 1917. Other Patents Pending. Will Remove Corks, Crowns, Milk Bottle Caps Etc. with a simple twist." To remove a cork, the tool is placed on top of a bottle and the pins are pushed down. The cork is removed by slowly turning and lifting. Turn slowly and draw out cork. Do it gently. To release stopper, pull pins up.

The U-Neek.
$1000-1500.

Waiters' Friends

When waiters open bottles of wine, the overwhelming majority will use one of these simple lever devices. They are a waiter's friend because they fold up nicely with the worm protected in the pocket. It can be quickly armed and ready for use by simply folding the worm and the neckstand out. In patents, the neckstand is given the technical term "fulcrum plate." The point on early version neckstands is described in David Davis's 1891 patent: "a means for cutting the wire on bottles . . . as all malt liquors and many grades of wines are provided with wires to better secure the corks from involuntary ejections." Some waiters' friends have knives on the backside for cutting the foil on the bottle. The worm is inserted into the cork, the neckstand is placed on the bottle rim, the handle is raised, and the cork is extracted.

Left: Cast mermaid marked "DAVIS IMPROVED" PAT'D JULY 14-91, FURTHER PATS PND'G, referring to a patent by Charles Puddefoot. $1000-1200.
Right: German steel alligator. $800-1000.

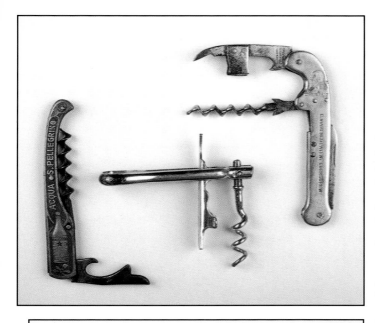

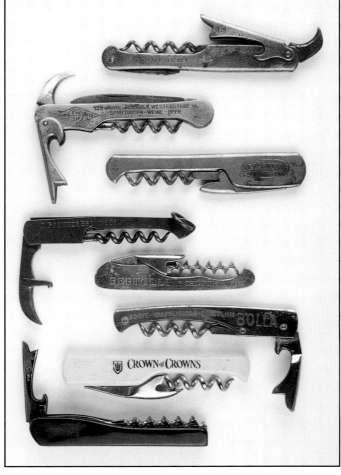

Top: *Left:* Ornate designs from Germany made this style a very attractive advertising giveaway. $80-150.
Middle: The "Universal," a 1906 American patent by Harry Noyes. A lever where the handle is pushed down rather than pulled up to extract the cork. Frequently found with advertising for Green River Whiskey. Less common are a plain version and one with advertising for Olympia Brewing Company of Washington. $50-100.
Right: An English waiter's friend by John Watts marked C. VIARENGO PATENT CORKSCREW, (man's head) THE CORKSCREW KING, RD. NO. 581553 (1911). $250-500.

Bottom: *Top to bottom:* Two waiter's friends with a single knife blade and a foil cutter. $50-60; Simple advertising. $15-20; Early steel beer advertising with two hook neckstand. $80-100; Four modern waiter's friends with various handles and advertising. $10-15.

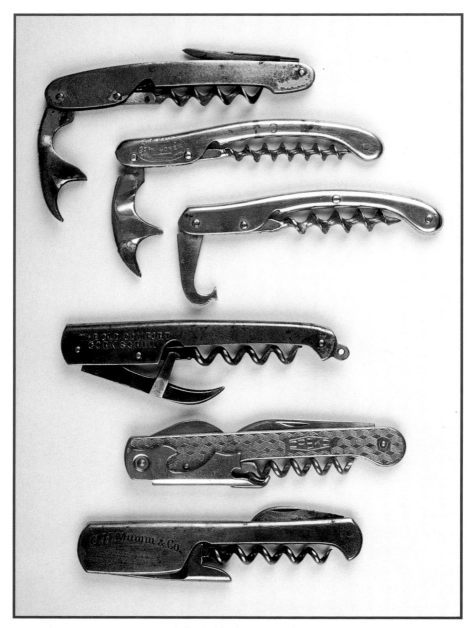

Top to bottom: Davis patent with knife blade on top of handle. $125-175; A "regular" Davis frequently sold to breweries as a giveaway with an engraved advertising message. $75-100; The Davis look with a Puddefoot neckstand. $250-300; "The Old Comfort Cork Screw." $75-100; East German "Dreko." $20-30; "G. H. Mumm & Co." advertisement. $75-125.

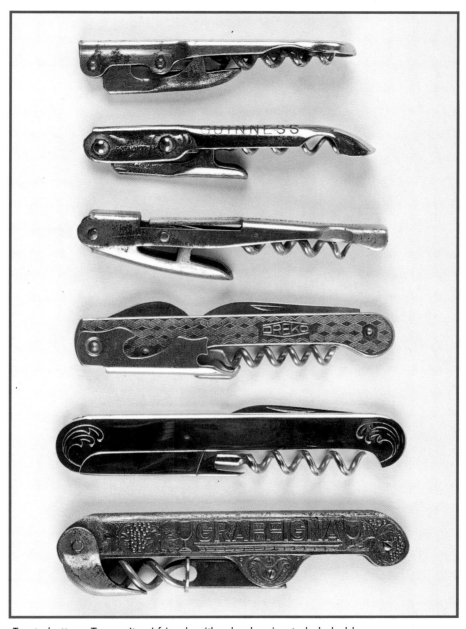

Top to bottom: Two waiters' friends with a backspring to help hold
the worm in place. Found with and without advertising. $75-100;
John Watts waiter's friend with advertising: "Creese's for Something
Good." $60-80; East German "Dreko." $20-30; Made with a knife
or can opener by Eduard Becker, Solingen, Germany. $50-60;
Marked CENTENARIO and GRAFFIGNA, this looks like a waiter's
friend, but the only function of the swivel piece is to protect the end
of the worm which is a double helix. *$Rare.*

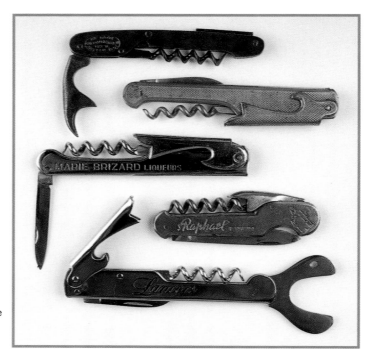

An assortment of advertising waiter's friends with single knife blade only. $15-25.

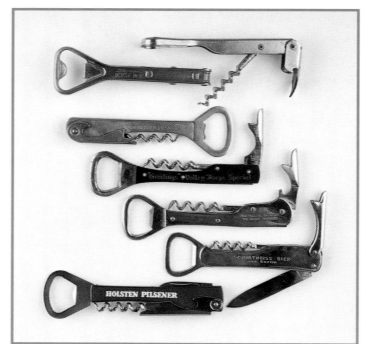

An assortment of waiter's friends with bottle cap lifters. $5-25.

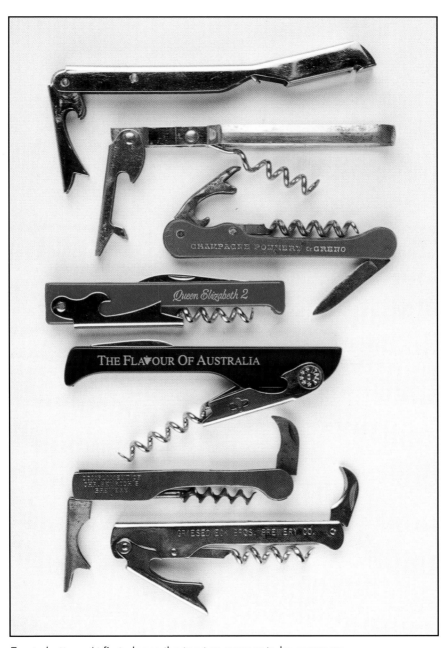

Top to bottom: At first glance the top two appear to be common
style can opener combinations. But the can opener is absent.
$10-40; Three with advertising on bright color plastic handles.
$5-20; Two steel with beer advertising. $50-100.

Top to bottom: 1988 Spanish patent "Puigpull" by Ralon Brucart Puig. $10-20; The "Maxos" from Japan. $15-25; French Laguiole knife. $100-200; The "Pulltaps" from Spain. $18-30; "Hugh Johnson's Personal Corkscrew." Currently sold in fitted case by the *Wine Enthusiast* for $39.95; The "Liftmaster" with chrome body. $15-25.

Walker & Williamson

Edwin Walker's Erie Specialty Company located in Erie, Pennsylvania, and C. T. Williamson Company founded in Newark, New Jersey, in 1876 were serious competitors for over 40 years in the North American corkscrew market. Both sold a variety of wood handle corkscrews with various worms and bells to companies from coast to coast for advertising purposes. In *The 1998 Handbook of United States Beer Advertising Openers and Corkscrews* by Stanley, Kaye, and Bull, there are 300 Walker corkscrews cataloged and only 60 for Williamson.

Left: Williamson's 1898 design patent for a cast iron wire breaker and cap lifter above cast bell.
Right: Wood handle corkscrew by Williamson with flat wire breaker above cast bell.
Values will range from $15-100 depending upon advertising content. Value with no advertising is $8-15.

Three Schlitz Beer advertising corkscrews *from left to right:* Williamson with cast wire breaker above bell; Walker with cast wire breaker on bell; Walker with cast wire breaker and cap lifter on bell. $30-50.

Left: Walker 1893 patent with foil cutter in handle. *Right:* 1893 Walker with cast iron cap lifter in handle. $15-100 with advertising; $8-15 without advertising.

Whistles

When it is time to call friends to the wine cellar to open a bottle of wine, why not use a corkscrew with a built-in whistle? A number of corkscrews have been produced to fulfill this need.

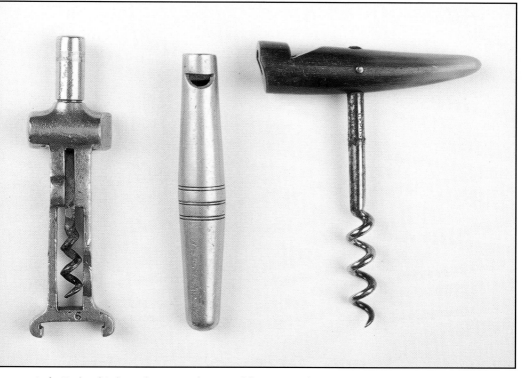

Left: Early whistle corkscrew with several functions. The worm folds into the center chamber with the shank acting as a cigar cutter. The top cover comes off to expose a screwdriver blade. The bottom part is used to remove shotgun shells. The grips are tapered so one side is used for 12 gauge and the other side for 16 gauge. $750-1000.
Middle: A roundlet whistle. Unscrew the two parts, pull out the worm, turn the worm perpendicular to the barrel, screw the parts back together, and open the wine. $300-350.
Right: Small French horn handle with whistle. $100-150.

Williamson's Opens Everything

The activities of the Williamson Company of Newark, New Jersey, are best viewed through their own comments in an 1883 catalog.

We beg to call the attention of our patrons, and all who are interested in the progress of American Manufactures, to the flattering reception our goods have met with during the past few years in this country and in Europe. Notwithstanding the established reputation of English, French and German productions of Iron and Steel Goods, we are pleased to announce that the introduction of our Wire products into all these countries has been attended with unusual success. The Universal Exposition, Paris, 1878, gave them a high Award, and the press throughout Europe unhesitatingly and emphatically accorded us credit for showing them how to make the *best* and *cheapest* Cork Screws in the world, which in the *'Land of Bottles and Corks'*—as expressed by one journal—'must be considered a boon of no small magnitude.'

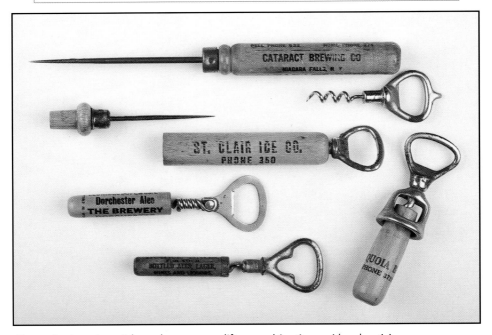

Top to bottom: Ice-pick, corkscrew, cap lifter combinations with advertising. $30-50; Rare combination corkscrew, cap lifter, and ice pick in which the ice pick reverses to fit in the handle. $75-100; English sheath type in the Williamson style with advertising and wire wrapped worm. $20-30; Another in the Williamson style with an unusual cap lifter head. $20-30.
Lower right: Williamson's "Power Corkscrew." A self pulling corkscrew with cap remover available with red, green, or clear lacquered wood tube. $20-30 without advertising; $30-50 with advertising.

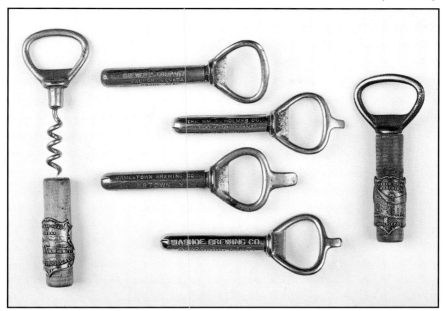

Left and right: Williamson wood sheath "Pal" corkscrews with decorative cast souvenir plates attached—"Marriage Place of Ramona, San Diego, Cal." and "St. Paul's Church, Norfolk, Va." *$30-35.*
Middle: Four metal sheath "Pals" with various advertisements. $40-60.

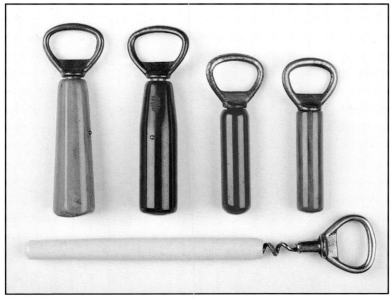

Williamson's "Don't Swear" corkscrew/bottle opener combinations in various colors. The sheath is made of catalin. The large chocolate and caramel color sheaths have a pin through them to secure the corkscrew. The worm needs to be turned in and out rather than pulled or pushed. $25-50.

Wood

One of the first corkscrews a new collector finds is a wood handle T-type. To open a bottle of wine, the worm is turned into the cork and is pulled out by grasping the handle and using a little effort. And sometimes brute force needs to be used to extract a very tight cork. The collector soon learns that more interesting handles, shanks, and makers' marks are more desirable. He can also expect them to be more expensive! A close examination of what appears to be a common corkscrew purchased at a low price may reveal a fabulous find.

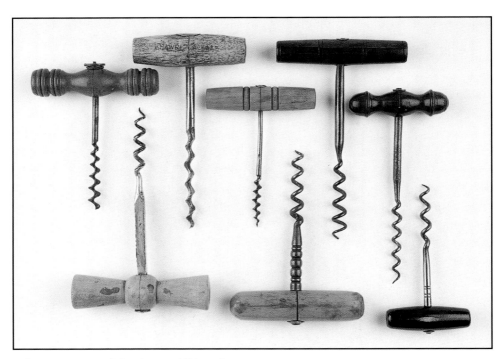

An assortment of simple wood T-handle direct pull corkscrews. $10-75.

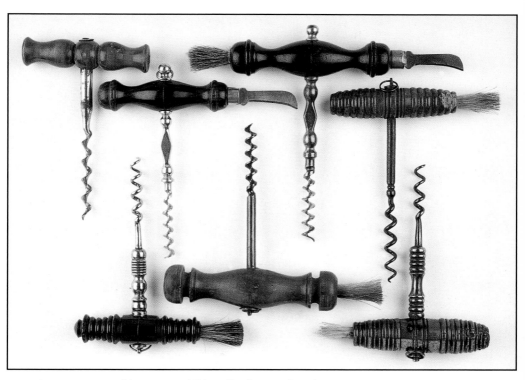

An assortment of better wood T-handle direct pull corkscrews, some with brushes and foil cutters. $40-275. (Those with foil cutter are at the high end).

Top row: Various corkscrews with buttons. $75-200.
Bottom row: Various corkscrews with cork grabbing teeth. $100-200.

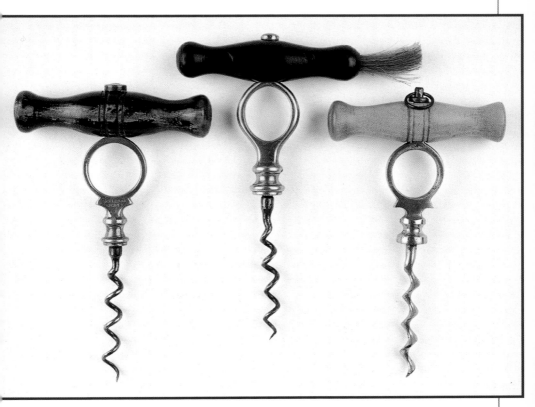

In 1876, Edwin Wolverson's 1876 English registered design added a hole in the shank for the middle finger when grasping the corkscrew. $150-300.

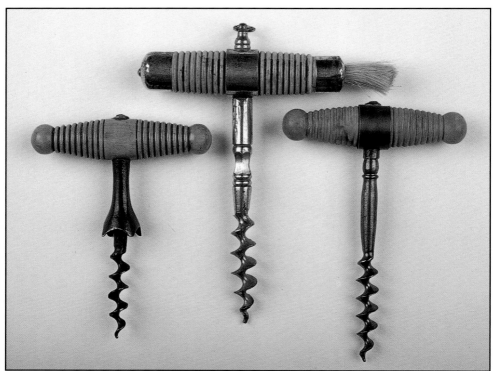

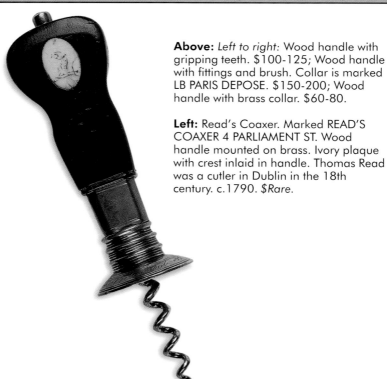

Above: *Left to right:* Wood handle with gripping teeth. $100-125; Wood handle with fittings and brush. Collar is marked LB PARIS DEPOSE. $150-200; Wood handle with brass collar. $60-80.

Left: Read's Coaxer. Marked READ'S COAXER 4 PARLIAMENT ST. Wood handle mounted on brass. Ivory plaque with crest inlaid in handle. Thomas Read was a cutler in Dublin in the 18th century. c.1790. $Rare.

Wood & Other Double Action

These double action corkscrews have been produced for many years and are still being produced today. Plain versions can be found in housewares sections of department stores and marked varieties in souvenir shops. With the exception of the "Club," many collectors shun them. A well rounded collection should, however, have a sampling of some of the better examples. Today's examples are often called the "Bistro."

Left to right: Wood marked COPEX MADE IN FRANCE. $30-40; The French "Club," 19th century, made of olive wood. $100-200; Black plastic imprinted "1977 The Queen's Silver Jubilee." Jubilee collectors might give the corkscrew collector some stiff competition for this one. $20-100; Barrel and wings carved from horn. Threaded shaft is plastic molded to look like wood. $30-50.

Just a few more . . .

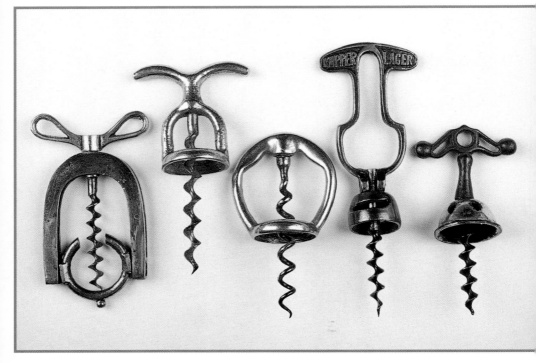

Left to right: The "Bonsa" 1899 German registered design by Julius Everts. $500-750; The "Pet" two finger self puller. $75-100; William Plant's 1905 English "Magic" patent. $75-100; Wilhelm Von zur Gathen's 1894 German registered design for a folding bell cap. $600-800; 1892 German design registration by Eduard Müller for a bell with mustache handle. $150-200.

Figural Corkscrews
Part 2

Anchors

It's a natural. Turn an anchor upside down and it makes the perfect corkscrew handle! Anchor corkscrews are most frequently found in brass with a friction fit sheath with a cap lifter on one end. In the best "T-handle" design, the anchor base pulls out with worm attached. The sheath then serves as the handle for the cap lifter. The less desirable types have a worm attached to the cap lifter, which is exposed when the cap lifter is pulled from the sheath.

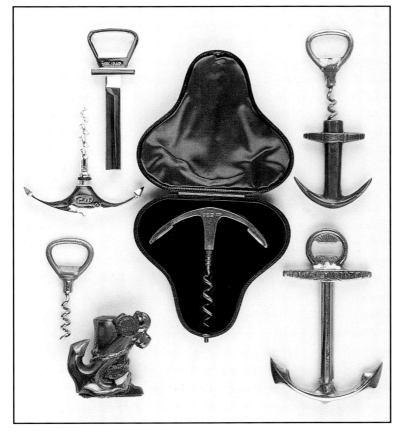

Left side: The silver plated anchor is marked UK. PAT and has the initials M H engraved. $50-60; An anchor lashed to a piling forms the sheath for the worm. It has a "Cape Cod" souvenir plate. $20-30.
Middle: An English anchor in velvet lined case. $200-300.
Right side: Anchor with friction fit sheath covering worm. $20-30; Marked H.M.S. VICTORY. $20-30.

Anri

ANRI figures have been produced in Northern Italy since 1912. The name comes from the founder *Antonio Riffeser*. Carvings produced by ANRI include corkscrews, bottle openers, bottle stoppers, humidors, salad sets, barsets, figurines, napkin rings, nutcrackers, cigarette boxes, calendars, pipe holders, pourers, place card holders, bookmarks, letter openers, thermometers, and toothpick holders. In the hunt for ANRI corkscrews, the collector will find some pretty stiff competition from the ANRI collector.

Above: The head of the monk on the *left* lifts off to expose an attached corkscrew. $30-60; The choir boy in the front is not ANRI. His head is a corkscrew and in the base is a cap lifter. Marked MADE IN FRANCE. $150-200; The colorful monk sitting on a barrel has a corkscrew head, a bottle with a cap lifter attached, and a mug with a cork stopper. $40-60; The monks in the cellar are one of many scenes created by ANRI with multiple figures serving as corkscrews, cap lifters, and bottle stoppers. A set of monks in a wine cellar is valued at $100-150.

Left: *Left:* Double standing figures attached to the base are a corkscrew and cap lifter. One is usually grasping the arm of the other to either hold himself up or assist his partner. $50-75.
Middle: The musical trio includes a cork stopper. $80-110; Single figures such as the gentleman with a bad hair piece have corkscrews or cap lifters attached to the heads. $30-50.
Right: The sailor on a barrel is much harder to find than the monk. $70-100.

Left: Some of the ANRI figures got drunk and can be found leaning on lamp posts. The head is a cap lifter and the lamp is the corkscrew. Some have a suitcase behind them which is a wind-up music box. When the head is lifted off, the music plays. Drunk with music box: $100-125; without music box: $50-75.

Right: The bartender figure has three foaming mugs filled with cork stoppers. His head is a corkscrew and there is a cap lifter towel tucked under his arm. $100-150.

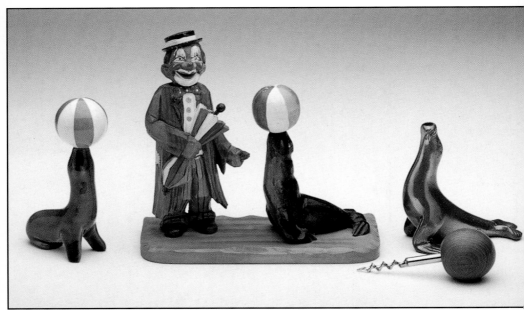

Middle: ANRI clown training his seal to juggle a corkscrew ball. The clown has a can piercer under his head. $100-150.
Left and right: These seals are not ANRI. The seal on the *left* is by Wade Pottery. $150-200; The seal on the *right* with wood ball is copper. $75-100.

Bar Bum

The Delsam Company of Vineland, New Jersey, called their product "The Lovable Bar Bum, A handy man for your bar." He is a 1950 American design patent by Samuel Gerson. His hat is a bottle opener, his ear is an ice or nut cracker, and his pants are a jigger. Removing the bayonet fit top reveals an ice pick, muddler, and corkscrew.

The Bar Bum in painted, aluminum, and bronzed finishes. $40-50.

Bar Sets

Barbershop quartets, round head kids, kids with hats, pilgrims in stocks, salt and pepper shakers, Punch and Judy, and ANRI figures are among the many bar sets produced. They are usually wood and consist of from two to four figures mounted in a wood rack. Wood racks may be in the form of bars, fences, benches, and the like. All too often they are seen with extraordinarily high prices and outrageous claims of being "unique," "very old," or even "one of a kind."

Left: "Koktail Kids" are a cap lifter, cork stopper, and corkscrew. The men are 3" tall from base to top of hat. $15-25.
Right: Pilgrims in stocks marked JAPAN. Corkscrew, cap lifter, and stopper. $15-25.

Bottles

One would certainly expect to see a corkscrew in the shape of a bottle. Many varieties have been produced and many have been used extensively for advertising purposes. Over 80 different advertising plates have been cataloged on the mini bottle roundlets alone.

Top row left to right: Suze Gentiane label. $50-75; A French waiter's friend picturing a Cointreau Liqueur label. $75-100; The Clicquot Club bottle comes in finely enameled and brass versions. The worm folds into the back of the bottle and the cap lifter drops down from the bottom. $200-300.
Bottom row left and right: Cast bottle advertising "Renat," a Swedish liqueur. c.1930. $70-80; Wooden stubby bottle. $25-35.

Left to right: French champagne bottle with hollow back. It has a folding worm, an over-the-top style cap lifter, and a champagne cork puller on the backside. $75-100; Copper colored pot metal corkscrew/opener set with Guinness Extra Stout label. $20-25; Three "waiter's friend" plastic bottles in various colors. A 1986 Italian patent. $8-25; Wood bottle with fixed worm and Bordeaux label. $5-10.

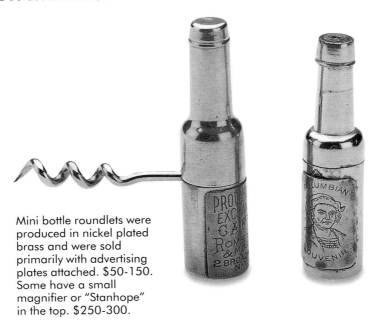

Mini bottle roundlets were produced in nickel plated brass and were sold primarily with advertising plates attached. $50-150. Some have a small magnifier or "Stanhope" in the top. $250-300.

Brussel's Spout

A block away from the Grand Place in Brussels, Belgium, one can find the *Mannekin Pis*. It is a small fountain statue of a little boy peeing. The figure has been fashioned into many souvenirs including pencil sharpeners, pens, knives, cap lifters, and corkscrews. The number pro-duced with corkscrews is mind-boggling. There is a size for everyone. There have been take-offs on the theme, including African figures, fishermen, and sailors. They can add a bit of fun to any collection, but they are neither old nor worth the stiff prices often asked.

An assortment of *Mannekin Pis* corkscrews holding worms with one hand or two hands. Values are $10-100 with better quality, more detailed pieces at the high end.

Bulls

There was no way you were going to get through this book without being subjected to Bull corkscrews!

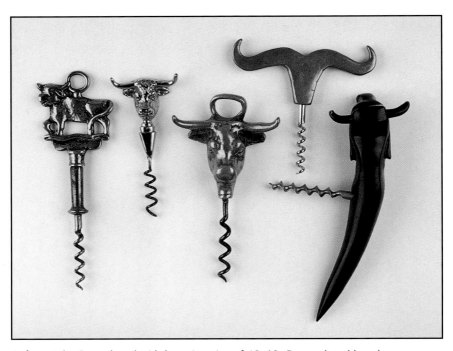

Left to right: Brass head with hanging ring. $40-60; Brass plated head. $30-40; Brass two finger pull with hanging ring. $30-40; Stylized steer head. $40-50; Part of a set including corkscrew and cap lifter. $50-75.

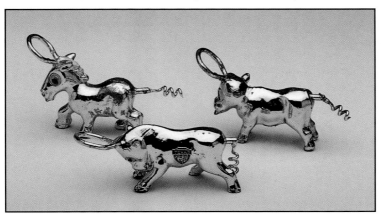

The charging one in the *foreground* is a bull. In the back are a horse and a cow. They are all cheaply made pot metal figures. $2-20.

Cats & Mice

Cats were domesticated in early times to catch rats and mice. The few shown here have been equipped to extract a cork while one continues the mouse hunt.

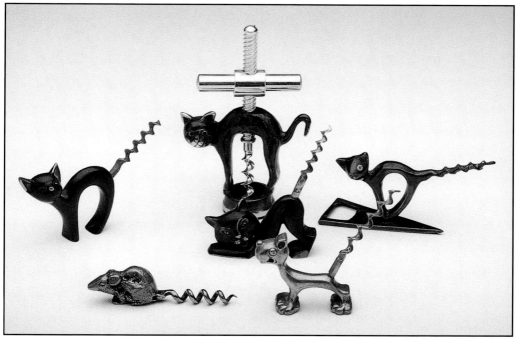

Foreground: An English cat, c.1933 ($75-90) chases a German mouse ($100-125).
Background left to right: Marked BALLER AUSTRIA. $40-60; Open frame glass-eyed cat with locking handle marked MONOPOL WEST GERMANY. $75-100; Copper finish cat with triangular opener base. $60-80.
Middle: Black cat made in Austria. $60-75.

Devilish Things

What the hell is this?

Top left to right: Black skull and crossbones with folding worm on back, cap lifter at the bottom, and hanging ring by Metalart Company, Providence, Rhode Island. Imprinted "Name your Poison." $10-15; Red devil clinging to a composition material bottle labeled "Champagne Foreign." $125-175; Red devil on a triangular cap lifter base. $100-125.
Lower left: Two sizes of a cork puller that one would leave in a bottle as a poison warning. $75-100.

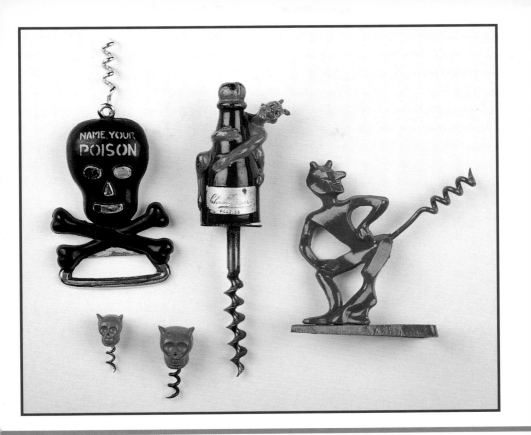

Dogs

Which is man's best friend - a dog for companionship or a corkscrew for wine? Owning a few dogs with corkscrew tails will eliminate the need for a decision!

A pack of metal dogs including poodle, dachshund, terrier, and a "Hootch Hound." $40-80 (except the German made Scottie with folding tail in the center: $250-300).

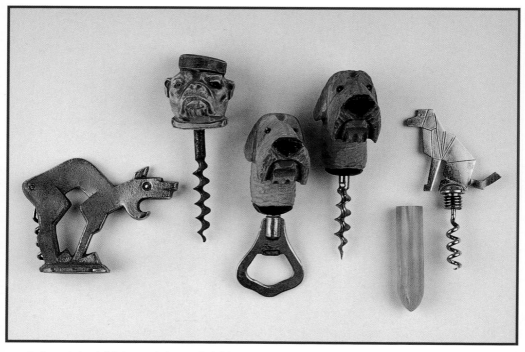

Left to right: A frightened dog with folding tail produced by Negbaur, maker of the common parrot. $150-200; A composition English bulldog head. $50-70; Corkscrew/opener set by ANRI. $30-40; Flat Art Deco dog with celluloid sheath. $150-250.

Fish

A fish swallowing a worm?
Now that's appropriate!

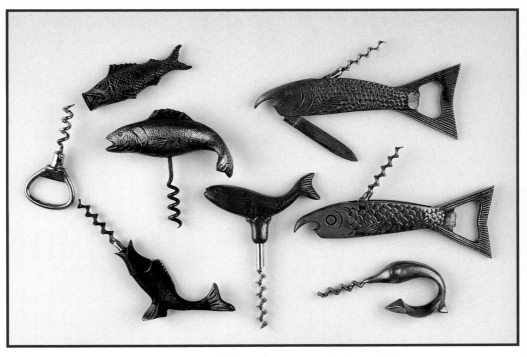

Top row left and right: The cast fish swallowing a worm is marked
JB. $50-60; A German fish with can opener mouth, cap lifter tail,
folding worm, and single knife blade marked SAKS FIFTH AVENUE.
$100-150.
Middle row left to right: Very detailed large cast fish. $75-100;
Pewter design with fish handle. $70-90; A cheap imitation of the
top right corkscrew without the knife. $30-40.
Bottom row left and right: Two free standing 3-D fish. $75-100.

Golf

Surprisingly, there are few corkscrews representing sports. There is a German corkscrew with a hockey stick handle. There is a series of Austrian Hagenauer corkscrews including an equestrian and a polo player. A series of French knives depicts basketball players, equestrians, and other sportsmen. However, no sport seems to have received as much attention in corkscrew production as golf. Many were produced as novelties and some as golf awards.

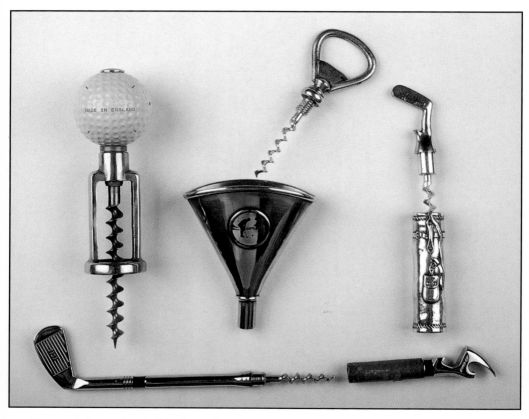

Top row left to right: Golf ball with frame marked MADE IN ENGLAND on the ball. $15-25; Wine funnel with corkscrew pictures of golfer ready to putt on the green. Made by Blackinton Company of North Attleboro, Massachusetts. $100-150; Golf bag engraved "Hook and Slice Club, August 9, 1928, Second Net." Also made by Blackinton Company. $400-500. *Bottom:* A West German well made golf club with corkscrew and cap lifter. $35-50.

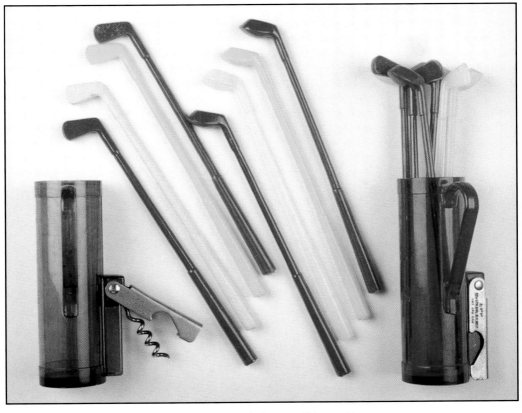

The complete "19th Hole Caddy" set includes a golf bag with measuring cup, bottle opener, corkscrew, eight golf clubs, and a "Pour Card" containing 18 drink recipes. The drink recipes have such names as Sod Car, Greens Lady, Divot Sling, Partini, and Swinger. The cap lifter folds over a plastic recess which houses the worm. The clubs are used as swizzle sticks. The bag is often seen in red and seldom seen in green. Some are marked EPP, 225 5TH AVE. N. Y. CITY PAT APP FOR. A set complete with all clubs, instructions, and box has the highest value. $10-50.

Horses

The horse head is very prevalent in corkscrew manufacture. Some of the sheath types have souvenir place names attached. As one might well expect, one was made for Louisville, Kentucky, the home of the Kentucky Derby.

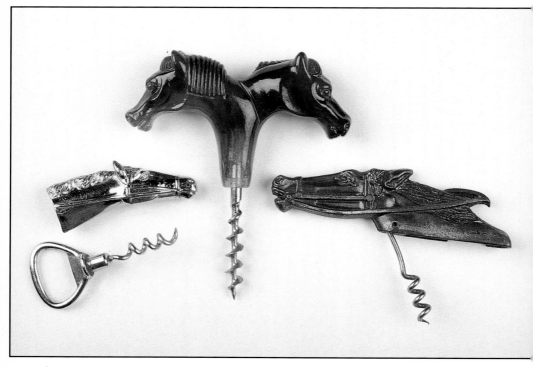

Left to right: Souvenir of Louisville, Kentucky. $50-75; Two horse heads molded in amber color plastic create a nice two finger pull. $90-100; The American made horse head with folding worm, conceals the worm when it rests upright on a bar top. $30-40.

Jolly Old Topper

The Steele and Johnson Manufacturing Company located in Waterbury, Connecticut, produced brass buttons and various metal goods until they went out of business in 1933. A 1902 city directory lists the company as manufacturers of brass goods for the plumbing supply trade, including screws, nuts, washers, bolts, chains and hooks; gas and electric light fixtures, including shade holders and canopies; work for electrical switches; and buttons—military, society, livery, and dress. There is no mention of corkscrews, but they did make mention of the Jolly Old Topper in their advertising as:

> *The Jolly Old Topper*
> His big mouth will uncap ale and beer
> He has big ears and perhaps looks queer
> Pull off his hat and you will see
> Just why it is that he's screw-ee

All three of the "Jolly Old Topper" figures have a wire helix hidden under their stovepipe hats. The mouth is a cap lifter and the ears are handles for the corkscrew. The bar accessories are cork stopper, jigger, and bottle top (a fourth, with a spoon, is not shown). $50-100.

Keys

A 1946 advertisement from the Castle Key Corporation of New York City promotes their cellar key as "The Castle Key, the smart accessory for every home" claiming the "design inspired by an authentic castle key." The advertisement shows it lifting a bottle cap, pulling a cork, and cracking ice. Paul Wyler applied for a design patent on this key in 1946 (granted 1948). The most common key corkscrews are those with a Verdigris finish with a grape and grapevine motif. Many are marked IN VINO VERITAS and many have place name shields attached.

Left to right: The "Bremer Schlüssel" (Bremen Key). The key on the shield has the same key bit as this silver corkscrew. $60-70; A silver key depicting four animals from the Brothers Grimm Fairytale *The Bremen Town Musicians*. $60-80; Silver key made by Napier of Meriden, Connecticut. $50-75.

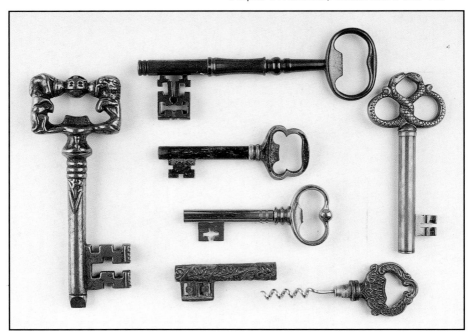

Left: A very regal looking key with sitting lions. Screwdriver tip at the end of the sheath. $100-125.
Middle top to bottom: Very well made corkscrew. Unusual because the corkscrew handle is much longer than on most keys. It goes into the sheath at the halfway point. $50-60; Marked M. I. GERMANY. $20-30; Brass key made in Holland. $20-30; Common key corkscrew. $15-20.
Right: Interwoven two snake handle. Handmade in Germany. $125-150.

Kirby

These corkscrew figures are commonly referred to as "Volstead." Many auction catalogs, newsletters, and journal articles have called the figure Volstead, but they are not Volstead! Rather they are a direct takeoff on the "Dry" figure invented by Prohibition Era cartoonist Rollin Kirby. Kirby's figure was of his own design, but, as with most artists' works, is based upon objects of the past and present. Kirby's figure is a combination of Moliere's Tartuffe, Dicken's Stiggins, Abe Lincoln, Keppler's studies, and his own vivid imagination. The figure is also labeled "Mr. Dry," "Old Snifter," "Little Snort," "Codger," "Old Codger," and "Topper." These are the *KIRBY* corkscrews!

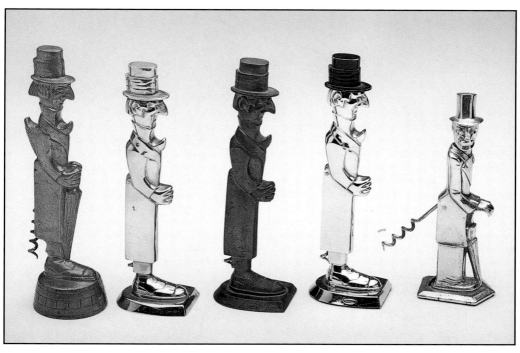

Many variations of the "Kirby" corkscrew exist. On the *left* is the rarest. This 7" brass corkscrew has cap lifters cast into the front and back of the head. Note that he is carrying an umbrella like the type with turning head. *$Rare*.
Others from *left to right*: A rare silver plated example. $250-300; Bronzed. $80-100; Chromed with removable hat. $75-100; The Schuchardt patent bears the closest resemblance to the figure created by Rollin Kirby. Marked MADE IN U. S. A. PAT'D and NEGBAUR, N. Y. $100-200.

Left: Design patent of Alfred Flauder. This combination bar tool has been noted in silver plate, nickel plate, and bronze plate. $150-200.
Middle: "Jollyfication Set" includes a cocktail spoon and a bottle shaped sheathed corkscrew/cap lifter combination. $100-150.
Right: Horace Bridgewater's 1932 design patent for a "Combination Bottle Opener and Dispensing Apparatus." The coffin is 6 1/2" long and is marked PATENT APP'D FOR COPYRIGHT 1932 inside the lid. $300-400.

Legs

The gay nineties legs are German patent 21718 issued to Steinfeld & Reimer January 1, 1894. A 1910 Norvell-Shapleigh Hardware Company catalog calls the legs "Ballet" and offers them at $14 per dozen. These legs have celluloid scales of high quality unlike the 1970s productions marked GERMANY that have plastic thighs and stripes painted in the grooves.

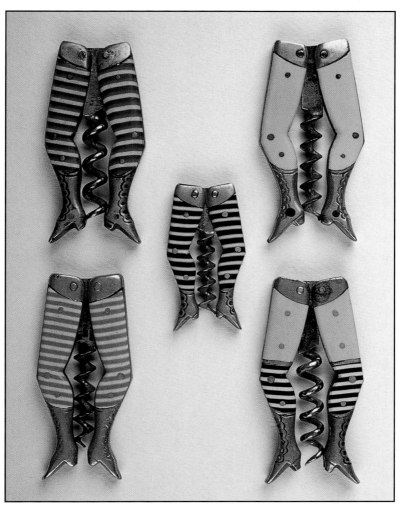

Mini legs are the hardest of the celluloid legs to find. The pair *in the middle* is 1 7/8" long. $650-850. "Normal" size legs (2 5/8") were made in many different color combinations and patterns. At the bottom of the value range are legs with pink and white stripe stockings ($250-300). Prices rise when a little flesh is shown above the stockings ($400-500). And when the stockings are completely removed and the celluloid handles are all flesh color, the prices reach their peak ($500-750).

Mermaids & Folding Ladies

Wouldn't the waiter prefer to grasp this Mermaid than the common cold steel tool used in restaurants?

She's a 19th century waiter's friend with molded celluloid handles. Or how about gripping the unfolded lady?

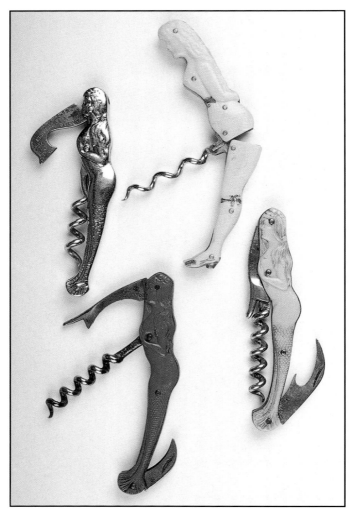

Top left: Cast mermaid waiter's friend marked DAVIS "IMPROVED" PAT. $1000-1200.
Top right: The woman folds in the middle and is marked GES. GESCH. $1200-1500.
Bottom left: Unusual reddish brown color mermaid with foil cutter on backside. $750-900.
Bottom right: Can opener blade on backside of mermaid. $700-850.

Parrots

In 1929, Manuel Avillar of New York was issued an American design patent for a "Bottle Seal Remover." A parrot without corkscrew tail is shown in the patent drawing. Although Avillar's parrot was produced as a cap lifter only, the version with folding corkscrew tail is most frequently found.

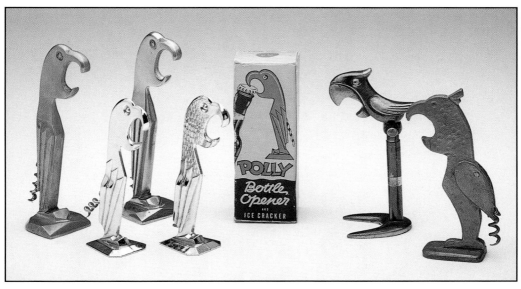

Left background: Two solid brass parrots stand 6 1/4" tall. They have a web helix tail. $75-100.
Left foreground: The chrome plated 5" parrot with plain Art Deco lines is the most common of the parrots. $15-25; Chromed with feathers marked NEGBAUR. $40-50.
Middle: The packaging for the parrot pot metal corkscrew reads "Polly Bottle Opener and Ice Cracker. Practical and useful. Bill removes caps, tail pulls corks, base cracks ice. Chromium plated." $50-75 (in original box).
Left pair: The parrot on the stand lifts off to reveal a web helix attached to his perch. $30-40. The crested parrot bears some similarity to the Avillar patent in the body design and cap lifter mouth. It is a solid casting with the wire helix folding between the wings and protruding out the back. $125-150.

People

Left to right: Huntsman. $70-90; Woman with toothache. $50-60; W. C. Fields. Frequently seen with matching cap lifter. $3-5; 6" Indian. $50-75; Smoking sailor. $70-90.

Left and right: Danish hobo carrying his sack of clothes on a pole over his shoulder, mounted on a marble base. The sack is the corkscrew handle. He has a cap lifter in his back pocket. $100-125; Popeye. A 1937 Swedish corkscrew patented in France by Bulls Pressjänst AB of Stockholm. $400-600.

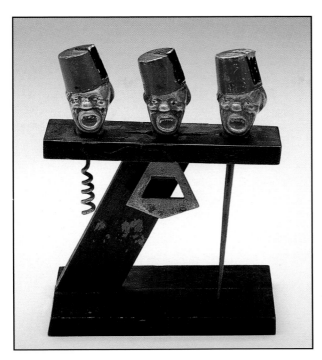

The cast aluminum "Men in Fez" bar set is seldom seen complete with original wood stand. $100-150. A "Black Minstrel" set (not shown) is even harder to find. $150-200.

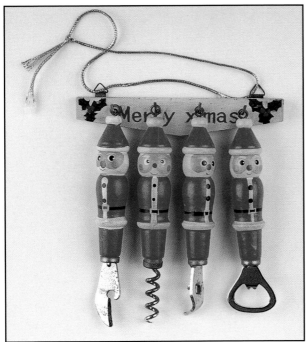

The Santa Claus bar set includes corkscrew, cap lifter, can opener, and can piercer. A 1950s decoration. $20-30.

Pigs

Who could resist the temptation to make a corkscrew using a pig's tail as the worm?

Top left: Pig's rear end has a bottle cap lifter on the other flat side marked COLONIAL CRAFTS PAT. PENDING. $50-75.
Middle column top to bottom: Pig marked with 1933 English Registered Design #779326. $50-60; Cast pigs like this have been found in brass plate, chrome plate, and cheaply bejeweled. $20-40; Howard Ross's 1949 American design patent. They are made of composition material and come in blue, red, yellow, green, and black. The snout is a cap lifter. $75-100.
Right: The standing pig with folding corkscrew tail was produced by Negbaur of New York who also produced Avillar's 1929 Parrot design and Schuchardt's 1935 Old Snifter design. $100-125.

Pipes

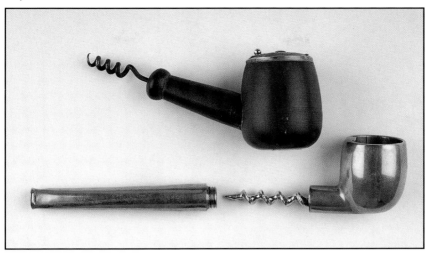

Top: Wood pipe with corkscrew tip and salt shaker in the bowl. $8-10.
Bottom: Brass pipe with the stem serving as a sheath. Cap lifter in bowl. Attributed to Architect and Industrial Designer Gio Ponti. $40-50.

Pistols

Perhaps the pistol corkscrews were used to open a corked Whiskey bottle? To get to the shot!

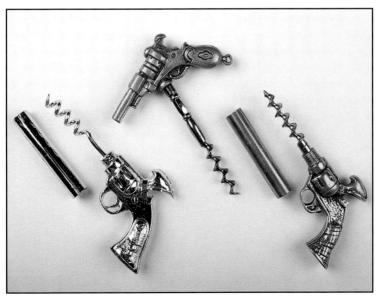

At *top middle* is a nicely cast revolver produced by Gagnepain in France. $400-500. These are currently being reproduced and, when compared to the older versions, a lot of the fine detail is missing. $100-150. At *bottom right* is a cast pistol with the metal barrel serving as a protective sheath. $80-100. The cheap modern pistol on the *left* has a friction fit plastic sheath. $10-20.

Sailing

Left: "What poor an instrument can do a noble deed?" (Anthony & Cleopatra). That's what it says on the leather fitted sheath of this corkscrew. It is a two finger brass pull with a hanging ring and really isn't too poor of an instrument for a noble deed like opening a bottle of wine! The ship is the H. M. S. *Victory*. $50-60.
Middle: A two headed pewter Viking ship with sail marked ZERO ($100-175) and Viking ship with head and tail with silver sail. $75-100.
Right: A two finger pull version of the *Victory*. This one comes from a set of three including cap lifter and bottle cork. $15-25.

Syroco

The Syracuse Ornamental Company (Syroco) of Syracuse, New York, produced corkscrews during the 1940s and 1950s. The corkscrews were compression molded with a composition of wood powder and thermoset resin. The worms and bells were supplied by Williamson Company of Newark, New Jersey.

There are three types of Syroco corkscrews: full figure with removable head to expose the corkscrew, head only, and a full figure (Scotty dog only) with corkscrew attachment. Some of the figures were painted, while others were stained with a walnut finish. All of the detachable heads could be purchased separately. The only full figures are the man with top hat, waiter, Indian, monk, clown, and knight. The collector should be cautious of other Syroco heads placed in these bodies or mismatched!

Left to right: Painted top hat man named in various catalogs Old Codger, Codger, and Topper. $90-150; Painted waiter. $90-150; Monk. $300-450; Painted clown. $350-550; Indian. $800-1200.

Left to right: Black and white Scotty Dog opener/ corkscrew set. $150-250/set; Police Dog. $75-100; Pickwick. $90-160; Laughing Man. $80-130.

Wild Kingdom

Here's something to ponder: Figural bottle cap lifters cast in the form of elephants and donkeys turn up at antiques sales frequently. Donkey cap lifters seem to be more commonly found than elephants. In corkscrews, however, few donkey figures have been discovered, while a number of elephants have turned up. Does this mean that Republicans drink wine and Democrats drink beer?

Left to right: Israeli donkey. $50-75; English donkey. c.1933. $60-80; A prancing lion with cap lifter mouth. Base is marked MADE IN ISRAEL. 4 1/2" tall. $60-80; Brass pelican. $60-75; Brass running monkey. $60-75; Brass elephant with wire helix. $60-80; Seated Austrian elephant. $125-150; Brass German elephant with folding fluted helix. $200-300.

Wood Carvings

A great variety of carved and stained wood animals can be found with a worm tail or a worm attached to the head and stored in the body. Some use the mouth as a cap lifter. These were made in France, Germany, Italy, and the United States.

Left to right: Terrier. $20-30; Growling dog. $20-25; French donkey with cap lifter mouth. $25-30; Elephant with wire worm. $20-25; Dog. $25-30.

Left to right: French squirrel. $25-30; French rabbit. $25-30; Danish mouse. $8-12; Dog. $20-25; French cat. $25-35.

Part 3

Knives with Corkscrews

Advertising

Knives of all sorts have been a popular means of advertising for well over one hundred years. The better the quality, the more likely the knife will be kept handy by the owner. The advertising message will be read time and time again. The corkscrew knives most sought after are the Anheuser-Busch champagne pattern pocket knives. Collectors of knives, breweriana, advertising, Stanhopes, and corkscrews compete aggressively for all types of advertising knives. Knives with missing or broken Stanhopes and blades lose a considerable amount of their value.

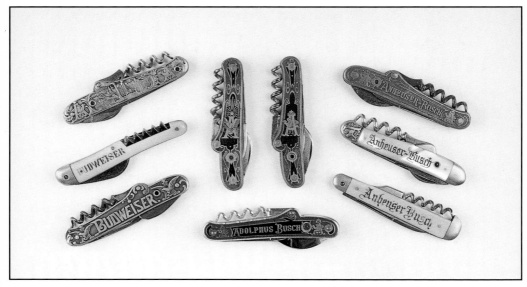

Over 65 varieties of Anheuser-Busch champagne pattern pocket knives were produced in the late 1800s and early 1900s to be given away by Adolphus Busch during his world travels. Lest he be forgotten, a photo of him was included in a peephole or Stanhope lens mounted in the knife. Some had a second peephole picturing the brewery. The oldest A-B knives have the "Eagle in A" trademark showing the eagle's wings spread out. Most of the knives were produced after the trademark was changed to an eagle with wings tucked behind the letter A. $300-600.

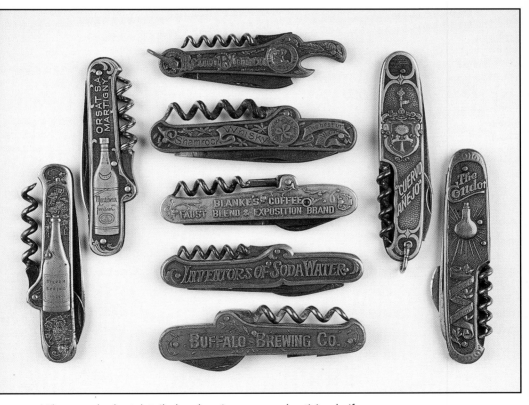

When you look at detailed embossing on an advertising knife, you do get the feeling that the advertiser probably made an excellent product to match his quality taste in advertising. Embossed knives depicting the company product such as the bottle with label are more highly valued. These knives include advertising for beer, tea and coffee, soda water, whiskey, tequila, cognac, wine, champagne, light bulbs, and even the gas company. $100-250.

Bottles

A collector would expect to find a knife with corkscrew in the shape of bottle. A collector would also expect advertising for wine on the bottle. It seems like a very logical place for a winery to advertise its products. Surprisingly, most bottle shape corkscrew knives have advertising for champagne, beer, soda, or liquors rather than wines.

Top: French waiter's friend advertising "Champagne Mercier." $200-250.
Left to right: Knife advertising "Orangina Gazéifiée a la pulpe d'orange" has a cap lifter at the top and a neckstand added like a waiter's friend. $200-250; An embossed bottle knife advertising Maggi's flavoring: "Für jeden tisch, Maggi's Würze, altbewährt." $250-300; French waiter's friend advertising "Champagne H. Germain." $200-250; Mother-of-pearl handles. $300-400.

Canteen & Picnic

The traveler who wanted to be prepared to eat as well as open a bottle of beer or wine had many choices. He could get an entire knife, fork, and spoon set including a glass, seasoning shaker, and don't forget the corkscrew.

The combination of a knife, fork, spoon, and corkscrew fitting together as one piece made a good travel companion. The simplest form for the traveler was one tool with folding knife blade, fork, and corkscrew.

Leather case stamped "Couvert de Voyage. Au Depart, 2S.Avenue de L'Opera, Paris" contains glass and utensil set. $300-400.

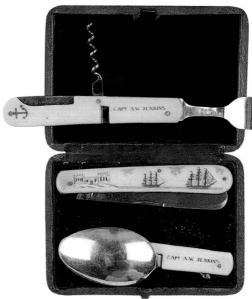

A travel set in velvet lined hard leather case. Decorated with sailing ships and the personalization "Capt. A. W. Jenkins." The knife blade is marked RODRIGUES, PICCADILLY (London). c.1850. $200-250.

Many utensils get separated from their mates either by loss, breakage, or collectors looking for only knives, forks, spoons, or corkscrews with no interest in keeping complete sets. The horn handle spoon and fork at *top left* is missing the knife. The set at the *top* is complete. $50-75. The knife with pinkish imitation mother-of-pearl covers in the *middle* is Russian made. $25-50. The other three are strays and are valued at $25-75.

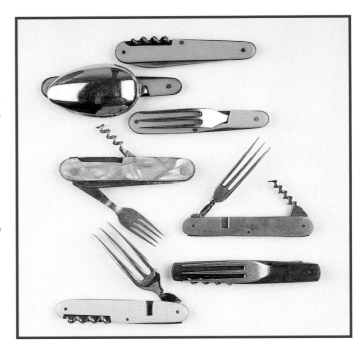

A 1914 Henckels catalog advertises the take apart utensil sets as "Army Knives." Knife collectors sometimes call them "Hobo" or "Slot" knives. The two or three utensils are connected by interlocking slots and tabs on the brass liners. They can be found with ivory, tortoise, horn, wood, silver, and celluloid handles. The worm is attached to either the spoon or the fork. Some worms fold out to the end and others to the middle. Values range from $150 to $300.

Decorative

Corkscrew knives with richly decorated handles with varying themes make colorful additions to any collection. They are works of art in their own right.

Brass handle knives with sports and music themes are French. Most are marked PRADEL and DEPOSE. Value range is $40-80.

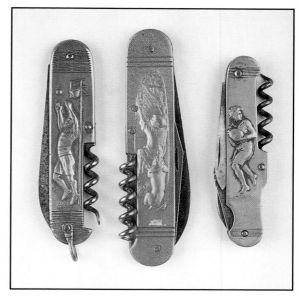

Left to right: 4" six blade knife with ornate silver handles ready to be engraved as a gift. $125-200; Spanish damascene pattern with one blade marked PAT. 52725 and another blade TOLEDO. $50-100; Bismarck manufactured by Gustav Felix in Solingen. $300-400; Wine, women, song—and corkscrews! They all go together so well! An Art Nouveau beauty posed on an advertising knife. $150-250.
Top center: Sterling handles engraved with "J. B." and "Wm Jackson, Rock Island, Ill." $200-250.

Diagonal top to bottom: Three women on bicycles pursued by three men on bicycles. $250-300; A high quality knife with blades marked REMINGTON. Finely detailed handles depict a woman at a sewing machine and the reverse has advertising "G. M. Pfaff A-G, Nähmaschinen-Fabrik, Kaiserslautern." $250-300; Ship with "Norddeutscher Lloyd Bremen." $200-250; Art Deco nude with sail boat on reverse. $150-250.
Right: Two blade knife with green, gold, and red handle design. $75-100.

Gentlemen's

"Men differ about politics and religion, and the girls they want to marry, but all agree that a good knife is a great blessing." That was early advertising copy by wholesaler Maher & Grosh of Toledo, Ohio. They offered elegant knives for fifty cents while stating "well worth $1.00." In advertising for direct mail order sales to the public, they suggested "Compare it with the rubbish sold in your store at 50 cents!" And, finally, in bold Madison Avenue advertising copy: "Jewelers complain because we do not ask $5.00 each for them; we would probably sell more to some soft-headed folks *if* the price was $5.00. But we are desirous of the trade only of people with good sense."

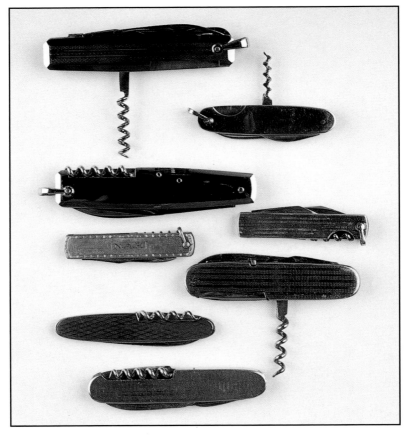

A wide variety of knives have been produced with handles suitable for engraving the initials of a friend or a special occasion. They range from a cheap single blade knife ($5-10) to a high quality knife with multiple blades from the French Eloi Pernet firm, one of highest quality cutlers in Europe ($400-500).

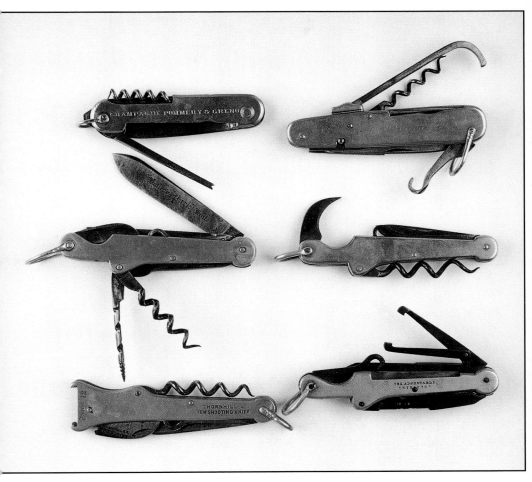

Left side top to bottom: French five tool knife advertising "Champagne Pommery & Greno." $100-125; Seven tools marked G. BUTLER & CO., SHEFFIELD, EN-GLAND. Master blade stamped "Butler's 'Park' Knife." $200-225; Westby & Levick's 1892 English patent. Marked THORNHILL'S NEW SHOOTING KNIFE, PATENT 12 / 16 and GRADUATING EXTRACTOR. $300-400.

Right side top to bottom: Eight tool knife with steel engraved handles. $200-250; Four tools marked ARMY & NAVY C. S. L. The C. S. L. stands for Cooperative Stores Limited. This was an English hardware retailer. $200-250; A seven tool knife with one end of the extractor pivoting on the other folding arm. Handle marked THE ADJUSTABLE EXTRACTOR with an 1883 registration mark. $200-250.

Korn's Patent

On February 8, 1883, George W. Korn of New York was granted German patent number 21125 for his "Korkenzieher." On August 28, 1883, Korn received U. S. Patent Number 283,900 entitled "Cork Turner." Korn's knife contains the "Cork Turner" having two "prongs." The long prong is carefully slipped in beside the cork until the cork is penetrated by the short prong. Four serrations on the long prong just below the point on the short prong engage the cork. A twist to break the cork free from the bottle wall and a long, slow pull will nicely draw out the cork.

The knife on the *left* is the "real" Korn's patent. It has the prongs pictured in the patent. The "cork turner" blade is marked KORN'S PATENT. The knife blades are marked HENRY SEARS & SON 1865 (the year founded). The foil cutter is marked REGISTERED. $1000-1500.

The knife blades and foil cutter on the knife on the *right* are marked HENRY SEARS & SON 1865. In addition, the foil cutter has the same KORN'S PATENT mark as the cork turner type. This mechanism is not shown in the Korn's patent. $500-700.

Legs

World famous French Laguiole knives are produced with wood, bone, ivory, horn, and man made materials. Blades are stainless or carbon steel. The pocket knife with corkscrew sells for $50-$350.

Many of the Laguiole knives with corkscrews have the appearance of a leg. Many other knives have been produced in leg form.

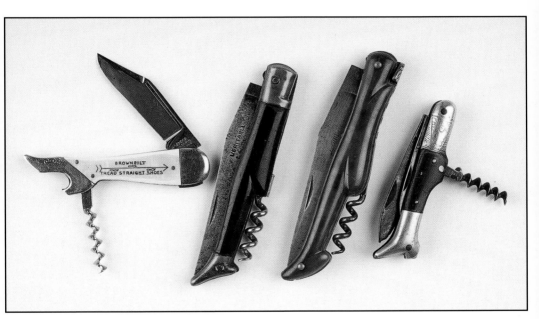

Left to right: Celluloid handle advertising "Brownbilt Tread Straight Shoes." Blade marked SENECA CUTLERY CO., UTICA, N. Y. c.1930s. $200-250; Black horn handle. Marked VERITABLE LAGUIOLE. $100-120; Red celluloid handles with Laguiole bee on the backspring. $100-125; Russian knife with two knife blades and a web helix. Long silver bolsters with wood handles. Dated 1899. $250-300.

Locking Blade

The master blade locks in place when extended. The ring is pulled to release the lock and close the knife.

Top: A stag horn split in two sections and mounted on full brass liners. The blade is marked HENRY BOKER'S IMPROVED CUTLERY. The web helix folds out of the curved back. 10 1/2" when opened. $250-300.
Middle: An early 19th century carved horn fitted with a master blade marked only A. T. and a web helix fitted into the fancy long backspring. $300-350.
Bottom: A modern bone handle with master blade marked J. M. NOGENT - INOX, FORGE MAIN. Also has a saw blade and a fluted wire helix. $250-300.

Mechanical

In 1987, the late Bob Nugent published his booklet *Knives with Corkscrews.* Bob had a great passion for corkscrews knives and spent hundreds of hours researching their history. He was fascinated with the many ingenious mechanisms employed to release the worm from the knife handle. These methods are illustrated and detailed in his booklet. Most of the inventions dealt with making the worm and shank as long as the knife handle to ensure greater purchase of the cork and gripping room for pulling the cork. The booklet includes worms on knives that slide, rotate, expand, hinge, pivot, and come out of hiding.

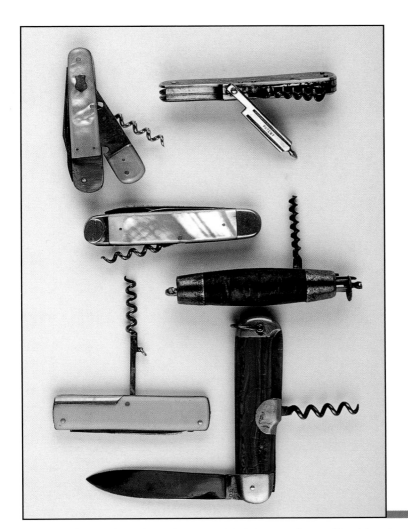

Top row: The mother-of-pearl on one side is in two pieces affixed to a two piece brass liner. The larger piece of the liner pivots and by pushing it up the worm is raised. $600-800; A three blade Swedish knife. The worm is hidden under a nail file. When the file is moved laterally, the worm pops out of its chamber. Reverse the movement, to store the worm. $700-900.

Second row: Two blade knife with mother-of-pearl handles. The worm is released by grasping the oval disks on the end bolsters between the thumb and forefinger. Turning the disks moves a pin that locks over the last turn of the worm and a spring forces the worm upward. $600-800; Swedish "art" or "barrel" knife, which is more frequently seen in a variety of sizes without the corkscrew. The knife folds into a brass case and slides into the barrel handle. The corkscrew pops up by pushing a tab at the top and then it is slid along a channel to the center to form a T-handle corkscrew. $800-1200.

Bottom row: In this 1908 German registration a small ring attached at the halfway point of the corkscrew is grasped and slid down a slot to bring the worm out. It can then be turned perpendicular to the handle. The knife has two unmarked blades. $800-1000; The corkscrew lifts up normally, but there is no fingernail notch for lifting the knife blade. When the worm is fully extended, pushing it to one side will move a spring to lift the knife blade. When the knife is fully extended, it locks and is unlocked again by moving the worm. Celluloid mahogany grain handles. c.1900. $400-500.

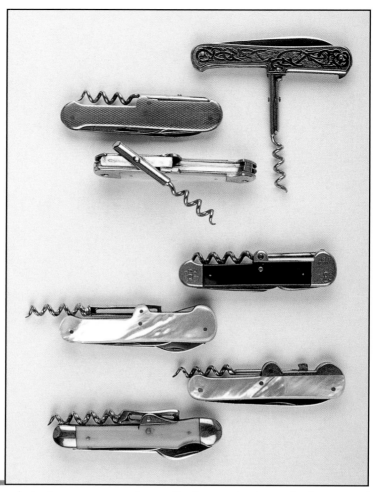

Sliding worms and pivoting worms were two methods conceived to make the worm of a knife as long as possible for more purchase of the cork and greater pulling power. The *top three* knives are based on Gottlieb Hammesfahr 1897 patent for a knife with a worm pivoting on a pin horizontally 180° on one half of the upper arm. It is then lifted into position. $250-500.

Fourth from top: In Carl Müller's 1896 German patent, the worm slides horizontally in a ring until a square form on the end of the shank stops it. The ring and worm are then pivoted into position perpendicular to the handle. A spring holds the worm in place when closed. Examples of true Müller patent knives are rare. The bolster is marked D. R. P. 89172. $400-500.

Fifth: Mother-of-pearl knife from Henckels, Germany. A version of the Williams patent (see *bottom*) in which the spring is mounted on the back of the knife instead of the shank. $250-350.

Sixth: A simplified version of the Müller patent with a pin mounted between the shoulders on the back of the knife. The shank of the worm slides under the pin and stops when its hooked end meets the pin. It is then swiveled on the pin and into position. $150-250.

Bottom: Alfred Williams' 1896 English patent for a knife in which the worm has a slotted shank traveling on a pin. It pulls out to one end of the knife, is swiveled on the pin and locked into position. A spring on the shank keeps the worm in place when closed. $300-400.

Miniature

Miniature knives measure in the 1 3/8" to 2 1/2" range. They were made as charms, perfume and medicine screws, novelties, and souvenirs.

Top row left to right: 2" with mother-of-pearl handles. $30-50; Jenny Jones of Wales. $25-30; Souvenir commemorating the 1953 coronation of Queen Elizabeth II. $30-50; Plain celluloid handle by Richards of Sheffield. $5-20; Australian distributor's name on the tang—"W. Jno. Baker, Sydney." $20-40.
Second row left to right: Ornate design with 1881 London hallmark and mark of retailer Walter Thornhill. Four tools including scissors. $250-300; A 1 3/8" miniature version of the Farmer's or Horseman's knives. Two knife blades, a wire helix, and a hoof pick. Perhaps made for picking the hooves of a Lilliputian horse? $60-80; Diagonal pattern with 1906 Birmingham hallmark. Scissors, knife blade, and web helix all on top. $200-250.
Middle: Plain silver handle with 1890 Sheffield hallmark and maker's mark of James Veall and Walter Tyzack. Blade marked with "Eye" trademark and WITNESS. Six tools. $250-300.
Bottom five: Tortoise shell handle knives with a variety of patterns and blade counts. $60-400.

Mother-of-pearl

Perhaps the prettiest knives made from a natural material are those made from mother-of-pearl. Knife collectors often refer to these as simply "Pearls." They are designed as elegant furnishings for a lady's dressing table, with accessories for the smoker, as special occasion gifts, for point of purchase displays, and for exhibitions. Pearls with corkscrews can be found with a single blade, two blades, three blades, etc. Look hard enough and you will find the number you want!

Top: Two blade knife with four pearl pieces laid in between silver bolsters. $150-200.

Second: A 3 1/4" pearl with five tools on the top, three on the bottom, and a tweezers and tortoise shell pick inserted in slots under the handles. c.1904. $200-250.

Third: 3 1/2" with two knife blades and web helix. Four panel pearl handle with decorative bolsters by A. W. Wadsworth & Son, Austria (1905-1936). $200-250.

Bottom left: Unusual shape pearl with eight implements. Note: All tools are pinned at the end, giving the user very little power to pull a cork with the corkscrew, but enough to remove a small one from a medicine or perfume bottle. 3 1/8" closed. $300-400.

Bottom right: 3 1/2" with master blade, pen blade, and fluted helix. Marked C. F. KAYSER, SOLINGEN. $100-150.

Stag

Antlers from deer are one of the most popular materials used for knife handles. They are commonly referred to as "stag handle knives" or in knife circles as simply "stags." There are hundreds of shapes and sizes. There are folding knives and fixed blade knives. They have been produced in Austria, England, France, Germany, and the United States for many years.

Top row: An American stag marked REMINGTON U M C, R3843. $200-300; Another American marked CATTARAUGUS CUTLERY CO., LITTLE VALLEY, N. Y. 3239H. $150-250; French stag marked NOGENT. $125-150.
Second row: A 5" German stag with locking master blade marked ANTON WINGEN Jᴿ, SOLINGEN-GERMANY. $150-200; English stag marked H. G. LONG & CO., SHEFFIELD. $150-175.
Bottom: A high quality German knife marked PUMA-WERK, SOLINGEN, MADE IN GERMANY, HANDARBEIT GES. GESCH. Nᵒ 5/5790, BESTELL Nᵒ. 3591 and ORIGINAL WALDMEƒƒER FÜR SCHALENWILD. $250-300.

Just a few more knives . . .

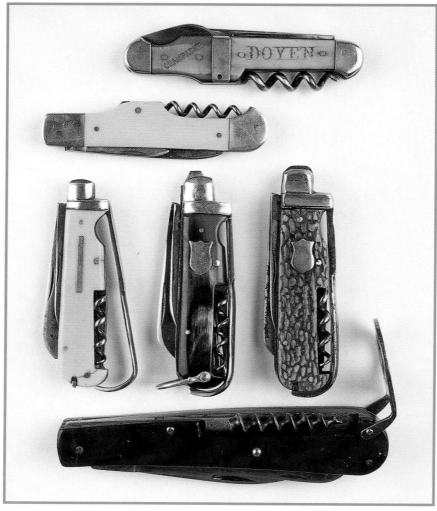

Top: Two ivory handle knives. One advertises "Champagne Doyen" ($250-300) and the other is marked S. MOLIN, ESKILSTUNA (Sweden). $250-300.

Middle: The Norvell-Shapleigh Hardware Company of St. Louis, Missouri, (1902-1917) described knives like these in their catalog as "Farmer's Knife; Length 3 3/4 inches; Polished Steel Bolsters; One Large Spear and One Small Pen Blade; Full Polished; One Saw Blade, One Horse Fleam, One Hoof Cleaner, One Cork Screw, One Gimlet, One Square Reamer, One Screw Driver, One Pair Tweezers and One Steel Needle; Iron Lining, German Silver Shield; Weight per Dozen 4 lbs. Genuine Stag Handle. $150.00/Dozen." Other catalogs refer to the knives as Horseman's or more commonly as a Farrier's knives.

These knives have two or three blades on top. Two or three tools including the corkscrew are under the hoof cleaner. A pick and tweezers are usually inserted under the handle. $200-500.

Bottom: Hardwood handle two blade knife with swiveling cap lifter on end. A saw blade is marked XVIII. $300-400.

Resources

Books:

Bernston, Buster, and Per Ekman. *Scandinavian Corkscrews*. Täby, Sweden: Tryckeriförlaget, 1994.

Blake, Philos. *Guide to American Corkscrew Patents, Volume One 1860-1895*. New Castle, Delaware, USA: Bottlescrew Press, 1978.

Blake, Philos. *Guide to American Corkscrew Patents, Volume Two 1896-1920*. New Castle, Delaware, USA: Bottlescrew Press, 1981.

Bull, Donald A. *The Ultimate Corkscrew Book*. Atglen, PA, USA: Schiffer Publishing Ltd., 1999.

Bull, Donald, and Manfred Friedrich. *The Register of United States Breweries 1876-1976, Volumes I & II*. Trumbull, Connecticut, USA: Bull, 1976.

Bull, Donald, Manfred Friedrich, and Robert Gottschalk. *American Breweries*. Trumbull, Connecticut, USA: Bullworks, 1984.

Bull, Donald. *A Price Guide to Beer Advertising Openers and Corkscrews*. Trumbull, Connecticut, USA: Bull, 1981.

Bull, Donald. *Beer Advertising Openers—A Pictorial Guide*. Trumbull, Connecticut, USA: Bull, 1978.

Coldicott, Peter. *A Guide to Corkscrew Collecting*. Stockbridge, Hants., England: Coldicott, 1994.

D'Errico, Nicolas F. *American Corkscrew Patents 1921-1992*. Connecticut: D'Errico, 1993.

de Riaz, Yvan A. *The Book of Knives*. New York: Crown Publishers, 1981.

DeSanctis, Paolo, and Maurizio Fantoni. *I Cavatappi/Corkscrews*. Milan, Italy: Be-Ma Editrice, 1988.

DeSanctis, Paolo, and Maurizio Fantoni. *Le Collezioni Cavatappi*. Milan, Italy: Mailand, 1993.

DeSanctis, Paolo, and Maurizio Fantoni. *The Corkscrew, A Thing of Beauty*. Milan, Italy: Marzorati Editore, 1990.

Dippel, Horst. *Korkenzieher*. Hamburg, Germany: Ellert & Richter, 1988.

Doornkaat, Heinz ten. *Korkenzieher*. Germany: Doornkaat, 1991.

Giulian, Bertrand B. *Corkscrews of the Eighteenth Century*. Pennsylvania: White Space Publishing, 1995.

Goins, John. *Encyclopedia of Cutlery Markings*. Knoxville, Tennessee: Knife World Publications, 1986.

Heckmann, Manfred. *Korkenzieher*. Berlin, Germany: Fasanen Edition, 1979.

Levine, Bernard. *Levine's Guide to Knives and Their Values*. Iola, Wisconsin: Krause Publications, 1997.

MacLean, Ron. *A Guide to Canadian*

Corkscrew Patents. Mississauga, Ontario, Canada: MacLean, 1985.

O'Leary, Fred. *Corkscrews: 1000 Patented Ways to Open a Bottle.* Atlgen, Pennsylvania, USA: Schiffer Publishing Ltd., 1996.

Olive, Guy. *Tire Bouchons Français Brevets 1828-1974.* France: Olive, 1995.

Paradi, Joseph C. *French Corkscrew Patents.* Ontario, Canada: Paradi, 1988.

Paradi, Monika. *Cookbook for Corkscrew Collectors.* Mississauga, Ontario, Canada: Canadian Corkscrew Collectors Club, 1991.

Perry, Evan. *Corkscrews and Bottle Openers.* Buckinghamshire, England: Shire Publications, Ltd., 1980.

Peters, Ferd. *German Corkscrew Patents and Registrations.* Holland: Peters, 1997.

Pickford, Ian. *Jackson's Hallmarks.* Suffolk, England: Antique Collectors' Club, 1997.

Pumpenmeier, Klaus. *Deutscher Gebrauchmusterschutz für Korkenzieher 1891-1945.* Bad Salzuflen, Germany: Pumpenmeier, 1997.

Rainwater, Dorothy T. *Encyclopedia of American Silver Manufacturers.* Atglen, Pennsylvania, USA: Schiffer Publishing Ltd., 1986.

Reichler, Mel, and Jim Egan. *Corkscrews.* New York: Reichler, 1996.

Stanley, John R., Edward R. Kaye, and Donald A. Bull. *The 1998 Handbook of United States Beer Advertising Openers and Corkscrews.* Chapel Hill, North Carolina, USA: Stanley, 1998.

Tweedale, Geoffrey. *The Sheffield Knife Book.* Sheffield, England: The Hallamshire Press, 1996.

Van Wieren, Dale P., Donald Bull, Manfred Friedrich, and Robert Gottschalk. *American Breweries II.* West Point, Pennsylvania, USA: Eastern Coast Breweriana Association, 1995.

Voyles, J. Bruce. *The American Blade Collectors Association Price Guide to Antique Knives.* Chattanooga, Tennessee: American Blade, Inc., Blade Books Division, 1990.

Wallace, Fletcher. *British Corkscrew Patents from 1795.* Brighton, East Sussex, England: Vernier Press, 1997.

Watney, Bernard M., and Homer D. Babbidge. *Corkscrews for Collectors.* London, England: Philip Wilson Publishers for Sotheby Parke Bernet Publications, 1981.

Articles:

Danziger, Herb. *The Syracuse Ornamental Company.* Birmingham, Michigan: Danziger, 1983.

MacLean, Ron. *The Common Corkscrew/Diverse Executions.* Mississauga, Ontario, Canada: MacLean, 1988.

MacLean, Ron. *Common Corkscrews II.* Mississauga, Ontario, Canada: MacLean, 1989.

MacLean, Ron. *Common Corkscrews III.* Mississauga, Ontario, Canada: MacLean, 1990.

MacLean, Ron. *Common Corkscrews IV.* Mississauga, Ontario, Canada: MacLean, 1991.

Nugent, Robert P. *Knives with Corkscrews.* Hillsboro, New Hampshire: Nugent, 1987.